life around the edges
a winding road…

TED DREISINGER

ISBN: 0692515933
ISBN-13: 978-0692515938

DEDICATION

For Molly, who continues to provide love and support when I need it most.

For Mariah, who carries the character, strength and compassion of her mother.

TABLE OF CONTENTS

ACKNOWLEDGMENTS

This second volume of work would not have been as easy to read were it not for the editing of my friend Frank Carmen. His sharp eye smoothed out the 'rough edges' of the manuscript.

To Jenifer Doherty (www.jeniferdoherty.com), whose creative energy designed the cover for this book, as she did for my first book: 'life in small bites – moments in time.' Her sharp eye and creative capacity reflect that 'less is truly more,' making the book cover attractive and appealing.

To Alexis Powers, who through steadfast encouragement in her writer's workshop, kept me on track for this second book.

Finally, to all the people and places providing experiences that touched my heart, inspiring me to record and share these small life stories.

INTRODUCTION
By
fp carmen

> "Enjoy the little things in life
> for one day you'll look back and realize
> they were the big things."
> --Kirk Vonnegut

Hello there...yes, you...the one holding this book in your hand, thoughtfully leafing through the pages. I was asked to write a brief introduction, so let's begin our book tour. First, how about that title...<u>Life Around Edges</u>...enticing, isn't it? Almost poetic, with a pinch of Zen thrown in for flavoring. And what about the opening quote by Vonnegut...too obvious? It just seemed to go well with the book's title.

In the few sentences just typed, I've given you a small taste of what you'll find throughout this lovely book of prose. Ted always begins a story with a short quote, a little spice that is intended to wet our appetite and set the table for the narration that follows. Ted writes in a light hearted, casual style about some of the people, places and things in his life and his observations about those experiences. The stories tend to stem from those more quiet, introspective moments that fill his day. Simply said, Ted pays attention to what Vonnegut refers to as the "little things in life."

Every life has its share of big events that help shape and define it. But whether viewed as a circle filled with family and friends, careers and conflicts, joys and sorrows, or is simply seen as a straight line stretching from childhood to old age, there is much in life that takes place along the way and around the edges. When a life is described, the focus is typically on the main events...the grand achievements, the joyous occasions, the bitter heartaches...but it's often the little things in a life that provide real substance and meaning. Like mortar between bricks, it's the stuff around

1

the edges that holds everything together and gives it shape.

Ted makes clear that there's much going on around the margins of everyday life. He tells simple but insightful stories about some of the happenings in his life. Along the way, you'll get to know Ted rather well. You'll find out where he grew up and about his childhood; you'll meet his parents and his sisters; you'll hear a little about his high school and college days, as well as some of his experiences while in the military; and you'll get a good sense of the man he has become and the life he is living. And oh yes, you'll meet Leah the cat, who likely spent a good bit of time napping on Ted's lap while the pages of this book were being typed.

What becomes clear, however, is that Ted's intent isn't simply to tell us stories about his own life, but to also draw attention to the fact that many of the most meaningful moments in any life take place off to the side, quietly and without much fanfare. Ted conveys the pleasure that can be found in the simplest of things, like a morning cup of coffee with his favorite cat nearby, while at the same time revealing the value there is in living a life that fully embraces everything from the main events to those minor happenstances that occur around the edges.

I refer to these minor random events as happenstance, some may call it fate or chance, but whatever the label, we can all look back on our lives and find those seemingly inconsequential moments, brief encounters or occurrences, that turn out not to be inconsequential at all. Only when viewed in retrospect, do these unanticipated chance circumstances disclose their true significance.

I first met Ted just over a year ago during one of those unexpected, "life around the edges" moments. We two just happened, by chance, if you like, to be seated next to each other on a crowded flight from Tucson to Dallas/Fort Worth, where we each had different connecting flights to our respective destinations...Ted was heading off to Europe for a medical conference of some sort and I was flying east to visit family and friends. A very ordinary occurrence indeed, but what was extraordinary, for me anyway, was that during the 3 hour or so flight, our intimate, enjoyable conversation never subsided and was frequently punctuated by laughter and more than a few "Really?!! That happened to you too?!!" reactions.

-- I read once that, "life is 10% what happens to us and 90% how we react". --

As is his nature, Ted had struck up a friendly chat shortly after I got settled in my seat, and although my nature is normally to avoid anything but incidental "small talk" when I fly...choosing instead to muffle the world around me with ear plugs and a sleep mask...by the time we landed in Dallas and shook hands good-bye, it struck me as I rushed to catch my connecting flight that I had just experienced something unexpected and a bit out of the ordinary. Even then, however, I had no inkling, not a clue, that a year later, Ted and I would be good friends and that I would be sitting here now writing the introduction to his charming book.

It was just one of those seemingly inconsequential moments that happen, a happenstance, but in this case, we both had the same reaction to the moment. When I sat down in that seat beside "some tall dude", I assure you, neither one of us was expecting to develop a meaningful relationship in the time it took to fly 950 miles. And here's another interesting thing I just realized...although we met out on the far flung reaches of our respective ordinary everyday lives, we are now part of each other's "inner circle". Go figure!

So, whether intended or not, what Ted does wonderfully in the telling of his stories is underscore how many of the small but significant things that happen in life often occur around the edges of the routine and ordinary...and when they happen, we frequently have no idea of their importance. Most of us can look back on our lives and find any number of major turning points or significant moments that, at the time, seemed no more than chance encounters. Ted enjoys embracing those little moments around the edges and as Vonnegut suggests, he recognizes their value and then he writes about them.

I hope you enjoy Ted's storytelling as much as I do...and, if you haven't already, that you begin to also appreciate all the little moments that take place around the edges of your own life. Who knows, you may even make a new friend.

IT ALL BEGINS AGAIN

"When morning gilds the skies,
My heart awaking cries:
May Jesus Christ be praised!"
- Original lyricist unknown
Sung lovingly to me throughout
her life by my mother
Fan Dreisinger

Mornings are my favorite time of the day.

They don't start quickly, because it seems to take a bit of time for the several million cells in my body to get in sync and wake up.

I used to sit on the edge of the bed in a semi-stupor for five minutes, as if waiting for the preconcert tuning of a large orchestra completing the tonal check of each player's instrument – you know, the confused sound somewhere between the scratching of fingernails on a blackboard and a band of cars honking their horns on a busy street – dissonant… irritating.

But then, the conductor raises the baton…a momentary calm follows and suddenly emerges the sound of music where the individual gives way to the coordinated impulse of single purpose…the many parts forgotten as focus and resolve become a singular, living thing.

For decades, that's the way waking up worked for me…the discordance of transitioning from sleep to wake…and then, in the space of five to ten seconds, the whole thing seemed to light-up…as if a group of engineers, having checked all of the internal routines needed for conscious activity of the day, had given the "…all systems go…" green light.

It is hard to describe the sensation, but it was a physically pleasant feeling, signaling it was time to get going, as Marcus Aurelius noted, to fulfill the tasks and duties of being a human being – meaning forward movement with the day and life.

In recent years, the methodology seems to have changed somewhat…taking a little longer – or maybe it is just a different routine, reflecting a change in the way I now live my life.

I suspect the internal engineers have sensed I no longer have a specific place to be every morning with clockwork precision…no clinic to open…no office requiring punctual presence…fewer papers that require 'immediate attention' to write.

Maybe they sense my life is slowing down a little, or that the tasks still occupying my time allow for more discretion on my part. Maybe they understand, that since my office is not more than a few feet from where I sip the nectar of the gods (sleep), it is not necessary to 'tune the orchestra' quite so quickly.

I suppose, having the discretion to choose what I want to do, and the places I want to be have created a calmer sense of the work necessitated by the 'engine starters' of my body.

So these days, I wake, not in complete stupor, but surely an early morning fog. I quietly trek to the kitchen turning on the coffee and turning off the house alarm. The iMac is next as it announces its functioning alertness with the 'bong' familiar to all who use this technology.

Soon, a satisfying coffee…that only my lovely wife Molly seems to brew 'just right'… is in hand and slipping into a comfortable chair, a book at the ready and Leah, our eldest cat – who by now requires assistance – finding her way into my lap, I am ready to peek into the mind of a writer, who through the labor of his or her gift, provides me the momentum to 'lift off' the runway for yet another day full of expectation and the unknown.

In truth, I find waking up to be one of the loveliest things that occurs with regularity in my life. Almost everything else I do still requires deliberate forward movement, whether it be regular exercise...weekly writing...fulfilling obligations for events placed on the 'to do' list or calendar...all of which are part of the process of life and require energy to continue to move forward on the journey.

BUT waking in the morning, ah yes, waking in the morning seems to be one of those automatic things over which I do not have input, nor control. Waking in the morning is a gift I find to be one of the great rewards of life...waking in the morning means there is another day into which I am privileged to meet an unknown future of conscious existence, and for me, it doesn't get much better than that...

FOOTPRINTS IN THE SAND

> "A man that hath friends must
> show himself friendly…"
> - Proverbs 18:24 - <u>Bible</u>

The Email

He was in sunglasses on the video, but the 'look' and the 'voice' were as familiar as my own image in the mirror. Although it had been quite some time since I had seen his face or heard his voice, in that instant we were NOT a couple of fellows in our 60s, but kids living in the 60s.

My First Real Friend

John and I were the most unlikely personalities to find resonance. I 'hid' from life in sports, he in the arts and 'we' in our friendship. How our friendship began is vague, but he was my first real friend – the one with whom animated conversations, ludicrous antics or complete silence fit like a glove. No judgments, no bitterness, no sustained anger but a huge mental bank account of tolerance. We were the fellas who hung together the way those characters in buddy movies do – he even had a motorcycle!

The last couple of years of high school, outside of the band for him, athletics for me, and our respective girlfriends, we were pretty much inseparable. . In an age filled with bonding chemistry and angst, and while trying to fit into a confusing and ever expanding world, our friendship flourished. We were a couple of guys who didn't get the world around us but were doing the best we could as we tried to figure it out.

You know exactly what I am talking about.

In youth, one thinks life will always be what it is. Nothing could be further from the truth. After high school we drifted apart to different colleges and different experiences - off to life.

What's the deal?
Growing up is the ultimate experiment. It was my assumption John and I would pick up where we left off. Four decades later it had not happened.

In life we get busy, distractions pre-occupy our lives. The quietness of an evening sunset, which seemed so crisp and clear, softens around the edges. Things slip out of reach as the days drift gently into the shadows of time.

As time passes in life, you realize in those moments of "…pale hushed stillness before the dawn…," you would give a lot to be that young man once again; you would be a better custodian of friendship.

So what do you say?
It is not clear to me how to express the meaning of friendships that men develop. We are not good at expressing our feelings to one another. We mask them through the many activities that act as replacements for expressions of deep appreciation and affection. We rarely tell them we love them.

You substitute…

There is a wonderful scene in the film <u>Dances with Wolves</u> demonstrating this very point. Near the end of the film, John Dunbar (renamed *Dances With Wolves*) is leaving. One of his chief rivals is *Wind in His Hair*. Because they have forged a deep bond of respect for one another, *Wind in His Hair*, couldn't bring himself to face '*Dances With Wolves*' departure. From a ledge at some distance, he called these most memorable and deeply moving words:

"*Dances With Wolves*. I am *Wind In His Hair*. Do you see that I am your friend? Can you see that you will always be my friend?"

It is said, "Some people come into our lives and quickly go. Others stay awhile, make footprints on our hearts and we are never, ever the same."

A fair amount of water has passed under the bridge since those early years when John and I were friends.

Maybe that video thing will work out. Whether it does or not, I know this:

"*John.* I am *Ted.* Do you see that I am your friend? Can you see that you will always be my friend?"

BELLS THEY TOLL

For what is your life? It is even a vapour,
that appeareth for a little time, and
then vanisheth away.
James 4:14 - Bible

"Tell mama what happened big boy!!!" "Please tell mama what happened!!!"

So began the funeral service at the end of that young man's life.

Barry and Benny…yes indeed…the Merchant brothers. I was starting high school in Fairmont, West Virginia – a small town nestled in the softness of the Monogahela Valley on the sides of the river so named. Fairmont, West Virginia, one of those small towns whose existence owed itself to the back-breaking work of bituminous coal mining. It was surrounded by some played out and some active mines along with the brick and mortar ghosts of what once were company towns.

Company towns…an appropriate name for institutions that kept workers forever in just enough debt to the 'company store' while inflicting black lung and other chronic diseases on the laborers for whom there was little chance of escape from the life in which they had found themselves prisoner.

It's funny how the ever-expanding busyness of youth brings with it a naiveté that hides from view things that, in retrospect, seem so obvious.

Different, but the same…

Barry and Benny were African American kids, living in the lines of demarcation that separated the black and white communities. Benny and I were in the same class. Barry, the elder, played basketball for the varsity team at my high school. He was one of the best athletes I had seen at the time, but he played primarily a back up roll. I didn't understand why in that day and only later realized this was due to a social discrimination related to "…the color of his skin…" not "…content of his character…" Those words had not yet been openly spoken…it was the early 60s.

I admired that Barry Merchant. He was quiet, thoughtful and had a twinkle in his eye. He understood, in a way I did not for many years, the role into which he had been 'caste' – pun fully intended. I spent a fair amount of time hanging out with African American kids in those days, and didn't understand then, as I came to understand later, there were certain expectations for me as well as them. I was oblivious at the time, and as I look over my shoulder, am grateful for my ignorance.

My father was a Baptist minister in this town – a minister at one of the more social churches. He did the things most pastors' do, and he did them well. He gave his life to the elusive woman of faith, and in doing so, helped many for whom life seemed simply too much to endure. Being a minister in this particular church was somewhat of a paradox, because while my father was white, he was an activist.

The circumstances that brought me to this particular day were part of the tapestry of my father's life and my emerging adulthood. In Canada, my dad had grown up from the streets. A tough kid who believed the underdog – in any fight – deserved an advocate. The first educated in his family, he carried with him this life history that had lead him to be a vocal and social activist as a youth, and as a minister of the Gospel. Wherever, in his judgment, there was a wrong, he felt obligated to fight the good fight. So it was with social activism of the civil rights movement of the 1960s.

Because of this unwillingness to be silent, he had become trusted by the African American Community and had been asked to participate in Barry's funeral. It was here I found myself in this little church filled to the brim on that warm summer's day.

Barry only had his driver's license for a short period of time when, for some unknown reason, he left the highway on a clear straight stretch, and ended his life at the base of a tree, even less forgiving than the social environment into which his birth had brought him.

This morning, as I wrote the words that began this piece, I once again felt the electricity and presence of a mother's pain and open sorrow as she draped herself over the open casket holding her son. I still feel the collective sense of loss amongst the community from which this young man had come. It was rich...it was deep...it was in an ironic way, healing. My father and I were the only white faces in a group of people from whom came a shared agony I had never known...open and vocal expressions hoping for some understanding as to why this young man had been so senselessly taken with no warning.

I don't know what it was like when these unanswered words of confusion and doubt were uttered, "My God, my God, why has thou forsaken me?" – A son to his father.

I do know, however, what it felt like when a mother cried and hoped for the unanswerable "...tell mama what happened, big boy, PLEASE tell mama what happened..."

THE LIGHTS ARE ON, BUT...

> "But the tigers come at night
> With their voices soft as thunder
> As they tear your hope apart
> As they turn your dream to shame."
> Fantine – Les Miserables
> The Musical

There is a quietness when nobody is home. The rooms once filled with activity, laughter and love – now curiously still. We are gifted, or maybe cursed, with a sense of sameness, a feeling of constancy in an ever-changing world. It helps us cope, providing a kind of internal security. In fact, nothing is the ever same...everything changes. It is easy to be fooled until you enter the house when nobody is home.

The guardian...

Riley met me at the door as always, with the wild enthusiasm of a puppy. Her ten years seemed to have done nothing to dampen her excitement. She looked quickly past me as if to say, "Where's Nance? Did you bring her? Is she still in the car? Is she getting the luggage?"

Nancy has not been home now for the better part of a month; she won't be coming home again. I had an overwhelming desire for Riley to understand her closest companion would not return. You often hear stories of animals so loving of their masters, they pine the rest of their lives at the loss. Riley gave me her best effort, but we both knew I was a poor substitute for that gentle soul with whom she had lived her entire life.

While Riley had always had a special place in my sister's heart, the last few years, as she began her unrelenting slip into darkness, Riley was her best friend. Before any of us knew the thunderclouds were gathering, Riley was there providing comfort with all her small heart could give. Before we understood the disease was robbing my sister of her life by inches…Riley knew. They ate together, watched television together, slept together, spending day after day in each other's company. When we struggled for patience in Nancy's circular, repetitive world, Riley did not! In the most tolerant of ways, she sat, with the rapt attention of a long lost friend, enthralled by my sister's disconnected monologues.

In the last few years, with minor exception, the two of them were always together. Getting Nancy to leave the house for dinner or a movie, without taking Riley, required all the diplomatic skill one could muster. Riley – the only constant in my sister's withering world…and now she was gone, leaving Riley alone.

How does one know what is right and wrong in these situations? For a second time this devastating disease had taken a loved one. Irony hangs in the air like a dense fog, as I recall how the girls and I labored over these decisions with mother. While all of us struggled, it was Nancy who carried the brunt, in the day to day management of Mum – before an assisted living 'solution' loomed large in her future.

It is said, "…if you want to know what's up ahead, ask someone on their way back…" The problem, of course, the '…what's up ahead…' is different for each person, each time. In some ways, there is no '…on their way back…' My sister is NOT my mother and this dance, while forecasting a similar endgame, is very different this time. Agonizing decisions…when they should be made, and with what right – the only similarity.

Under the angst of the day-to-day decision making process, these are the broad-brush strokes that haunt the soul. From the moral perspective, when one sees the decline of thought and function through the intimate knowing and loving perspective, and before God…when is it right to take the reins?

The flight from the West was without incident as it has been every six weeks or so over the past couple of years. The tornado warnings so frequent in this part of the world, lifted just long enough to make a safe landing into St. Louis. The drive to Jefferson City was without incident, and I arrived as so often before.

My dear sister, of course, was not there. She is now under the care of an assisted living facility and I will see her today for the first time since being with her in her home, a scant few weeks ago.

"There is a quietness when nobody is home…nothing is ever same…everything changes. It is easy to be fooled until you enter the house when nobody is home."

THEY COME WHEN YOU NEED 'EM MOST

"The skipping stone passing across the pond of time
touched my heart as it made its way to eternity."
- Anonymous

Nancy is never far from my mind…the voice, the humor, the quiet and not so quiet moments…yeah, that girl is never far from my mind…

Reaching back…

The letter began, "To the eminently religious lady and holy daughter Sapida, Augustine sends greeting in the Lord." The exact date is unknown, but it was written sometime around 429AD.

Sapida had lost her brother for whom she had made a tunic. He died before receiving it, so she sent it to Bishop Augustine, who seldom accepted gifts because he felt it was important not to draw attention to himself. In this case, he made an exception writing, "… lest I should increase the grief of one who needs, as I perceive, much rather to be comforted by me;"

He continued,

"…apply yourself, I beseech you, to far better and far greater consolations, in order that the cloud which, through human weakness, gathers darkness closely round your heart, may be dissipated by the words of divine authority; and, at all times, so live that you may live with your brother, since he has so died that he lives still."

Augustine brought a loving tenderness to this woman's sorrow, and

16

ended his letter by reminding her that through faith, her brother need not be far from her, with her love for him remaining embedded in her heart.

Threads connect…

Henry Scott Holland was a Theologian at Oxford University and had, among many other writers, studied St. Augustine.

In 1910, he became Regius (Latin for 'Royal') Professor of Divinity. In May of that year King Edward VII died, and influenced by the letter from St. Augustine to Sapida, he preached a sermon containing a poem he had written.

"Death is nothing at all. It does not count. I have only slipped away into the next room. Nothing has happened. Everything remains exactly as it was. I am I, and you are you, and the old life that we lived so fondly together is untouched, unchanged. Whatever we were to each other, that we are still. Call me by the old familiar name. Speak of me in the easy way which you always used. Put no difference into your tone. Wear no forced air of solemnity or sorrow. Laugh as we always laughed at the little jokes that we enjoyed together. Play, smile, think of me, pray for me. Let my name be ever the household word that it always was. Let it be spoken without an effort, without the ghost of a shadow upon it. Life means all that it ever meant. It is the same as it ever was. There is absolute and unbroken continuity. What is this death but a negligible accident? Why should I be out of mind because I am out of sight? I am but waiting for you, for an interval, somewhere very near, just round the corner. All is well. Nothing is hurt; nothing is lost. One brief moment and all will be as it was before. How we shall laugh at the trouble of parting when we meet again!"

Reaching forward…

My friend Lizzie had been touched by this piece and thought to send it to me. It came on a day when my late sister Nancy was in my thoughts and heart. It came at a time when it was exactly what I needed to read and 'hear.' It came, I believe, because there was a need and that need was 'felt' and answered.

It would be a stretch to suggest Augustine's letter that so touched Holland…so touched my friend Lizzie…so touched me, had a historical purpose for the moment in time when my heart was heavy. It would NOT be a stretch to suggest when minds open themselves to be led, the God of the universe can exert His will for the betterment within the shared community of His creatures.

Sapida wrote…Augustine listened
Augustine wrote…Holland listened
Holland wrote…Lizzie listened
Lizzie wrote….

and benefit was attributed to all.

Sometimes in the apparently chaotic nature of all that is, we get glimpses of the indefinable order that comes because it seems that God watches us out of the corner of His eye to soothe the troubled soul.

"Yeah, that girl is never far from my mind…"

WHAT HE DID'NT SAY

"Teach your children well,
Their father's hell did slowly go by,
And feed them on your dreams
The one they picked, the one you'll know by."
- Crosby, Stills, Nash & Young

Standing in line with the tremors of Parkinson's, his head was bent forward, arms trembling, shoulders bobbing in a rhythmic cyclic movement. A mask-like expression hid his humanity, the shuffling gait so often requiring deliberate thought, all were part of this debilitating disorder.

Disorder - "A physical condition in which there is a disturbance of normal functioning" – Webster…a disorder for the entire world to see, expressing the humiliation – the hallmark of the palsy. I didn't know this man, but in that moment, he was my father.

As a youngster, long before becoming a minister, my dad was brought up in the post WWI years, a time with little but hope and faith that tomorrow would be a better day. He understood the brutality of a lower-class life, the disappointments of hunger, and the humility of a youngster living on the edge of poverty. Yet he aspired to much more.

He did have help - the tenacious love of a mother, who lost her father and most of her brothers to alcoholism. Nonetheless, Martha instilled in her children, the three most important things a parent can give – "…faith, hope, love; but the greatest of these is love." Neither the scriptures nor age help in understanding the importance of these life-promoting and sustaining basics.

There is comfort in structure

My father's family found comfort in their faith...the black and white texture of Pentecostal Fundamentalism. Fortunately, Dad had a quick inquisitive mind, an ear for learning musical instruments; a resonant speaking and singing voice, and the good looks of a film star. These gifts fit well into, and were nurtured by, his Pentecostal faith.

Unfortunately, an inquisitive mind has little place in the structure of fundamentalist thought and rigid religious ideology. Unquestioning obedience is the bread and butter of unyielding systems of belief.

It is the refuge into which many retreat, and it provides the 'sanctuary of certainty' in a world seemingly otherwise uncertain. It provides a sense of spiritual superiority in a culture where success and meaning is deeply tied to external achievement. It provides confident answers, a community of faith that keeps one safe in the womb of God's eternal love and future reward.

It is also a place of stagnant solace where doctrine is the only truth. The apologist reigns supreme and dogma most often trumps rational thought. It is a place where physical infirmity is because of sins before God – a place where significant illness is a curse. Not openly discussed, it is the fodder for curiosity – '...what must this poor soul have done to be cursed in this manner...'

Don't ask – can't tell...

This is where my father learned his faith, but it was not a place he could remain because of his sincere interest in spiritual issues. His welcome slipped away in direct proportion to the number of questions he asked his elders. "Some day, you will have all your questions answered – when you get to Heaven, but not while you are in this life." This was not good enough for him. A promised future reward couldn't satisfy his restless soul.

At this juncture one reaches a crossroads. Move to a life of the world, where anything goes, where they have little to protect themselves from perspectives not taught? Reject faith all together, for if truth is not in the body from which they have come, is there truth at all? Or do they continue to believe that God has a plan with a meaningful impact, both in their lives and the lives of those with whom they come in contact?.

Curses – fortunately not foiled!

Leaving the 'culture of the church' often carries significant penalty. It can be mild ostracism or complete rejection, an expression of God's curse on the apostate. The latter is what happened to my father.

He was a resilient and curious man, understanding his true escape was through the door of education. He fought and struggled to be the first in his family to graduate from university – an anathema to his former spiritual mentors.

He not only raised a family, but spent tens of thousands of hours counseling the downtrodden, ministering to the ill and dying, studying each day, and preparing thoughtful/provocative sermons on a weekly basis. No canned homilies for him. It was prayer and arduous "digging the ditch" weekly to share his thought and inspiration with his flock.

If not always with the family, surely with others, he lived by the construct of two loves in his life – '…God, and the person in front of him at any particular moment...'

What he didn't do...
My father did NOT do the thing most of people in his position would have done.
- He did NOT burden his children with the punishing guilt of fundamental Christian thought.
- He did NOT warn against the ways of the world, using the eternal damnation as the sting of sin.
- He did NOT teach a 'fire escape' Creator who legislated punishment as a way of garnering love.
- He did NOT teach his children they were inescapably sinful creatures wallowing through a lifetime of sin, only to be released at death.

The gift
This gift of omission is more than I can express in words. Why? Because - in spite of his education, spiritual hunger and curiosity for the creative universe, he never escaped the sense that the Parkinson's was placed upon him for a sin committed in his early years. It haunted him to the end of his life.

His sacrifice was not just to those for whom he ministered faith, hope and love. For, if any of us has a purpose in life, let it be that we work to instill these characteristics, not just in our children, but in all with whom we come in contact.

He ministered faith, hope and love, and his lesson to us was to instill

21

those characteristics in our children and others.

What a true blessing...
My father's greatest gifts were:

- What he did NOT say
- What he did NOT minister to his children – fear of the universal Creator
- What he did NOT plant in our minds.

He understood what you place in the mind of a child may remain consciously or unconsciously for a lifetime.

What he didn't say allowed his children to Love God openly and fearlessly – a gift beyond measure!

You see, WORDS DO MATTER – even the ones you don't speak!

WHO IS THE LUCKY ONE?

> But I tell you, a cat needs a name that's particular,
> A name that's peculiar, and more dignified,
> Else how can he keep up his tail perpendicular,
> Or spread out his whiskers, or cherish his pride?
> - TS Eliot 'The naming of Cats'

We call her Leah because she is lucky.

In the Old Testament, there were a couple of sisters…Leah and Rachel. Jacob was a fellow who loved Rachel, so he made a deal with Laban, her father, for her hand.

The deal? He would work seven years for Laban and in return get Rachel for his wife - now that is love!

The day finally came and the marriage occurred, unfortunately for Jacob, when he awoke in the morning he found it was Leah by his side, NOT Rachel who he loved. When confronting Laban, he was told that Leah was the older sister and needed a husband.

Jacob ended up working another seven years for Rachel, but the point here is that Leah was lucky. She was lucky to get a husband, lucky to have children, and by her luck, she became part of the matriarchy of the house of Israel.

I mentioned "We call her Leah, because she is lucky!" This is because we have a Leah in our household too - that would be Leah the cat. She is lucky because she found us, or rather we found her.

Her mother was a female of questionable character and had a somewhat loose living arrangement with our next-door neighbors. The mother was an outdoorser, a mouser with a generalized independent flair both in character and apparently her occasional choice in male cats, meaning in the words of Crosby, Nash, Stills and Young, "If you can't be with the one you love…" well, you know the rest – okay, if you are under the age of 50 the line ends, "…love the one you're with."

Leah was so tiny when we got her; she fit in the palm of my hand – so tiny that she could hide in or behind my shoes. A calico, and as is often the case in kittens, her eyes were disproportionately large for her face and body. This is almost 15 years ago by now.

Three cats reside in our home, but there is only one who attends much to me. That would be Leah. Early in the mornings, she wakes me slipping into bed and climbing on board.

There she sits until I roll over on to my back, dancing like one of those loggers who stay atop a spinning log in the water. Once I have gotten to my back, she settles in with a gentle purr.

This, of course in her world, is simply foreplay for breakfast, you know – the tease. She has a clock in her head that says, "Okay that's enough. Now that I have your loving attention – let's eat!"

Some people say a person has only so many heartbeats in their lifetime. Leah seems to have a certain allotment of purring breaths before it's time to woo me to get her breakfast.

If I feed her and then head back to bed for a few moments – an infrequent event – she will return to my chest, lie down and purr some more, with a satisfied and relaxed posture that says, "Now isn't this better on a full stomach?"

There is something primal and exceedingly satisfying about lying tummy-to-tummy, chest-to-chest, heart-to-heart and breath-to-breath in the darkened and early morning hours. There is something comforting about lying there with a creature in whom there is no malice. There is something energizing about sharing a moment without words that satisfies both creatures in ways they find individual comfort.

This morning was one of those times. As we quietly lay tummy to tummy – me reading, she digesting and purring – we found a moment of contentment that these words fail to adequately express, and I was taken by the warmest and gentlest of thoughts that I was the 'lucky one.'

EMBRACE THE MOMENTS

"Time spent with cats is never wasted."
- Sigmund Freud

The years have taken a toll on my girl Leah. What was once a spry, take charge and by the way no prisoners feline, is now an older gal with a spontaneously fused sacral spine from arthritis, causing slower movement and a lot more rest in the day than in previous years.

On the day of this post, the planet has rotated 24,872 times since my birth and 5,838 for her. Skipping the math, and for clarification, I am 68 and she a 'gnat's eyelash' short of 16.

Cat's lives, as it turns out, are calculated differently.

According to Tracie Hotchner, author of the Cat Bible:

- 1-month-old kitten = 6-month-old human baby
- 3-month-old kitten = 4-year-old child
- A 1-year-old cat has reached adulthood, the equivalent of
  18 human years
- 2 human years = 24 cat years
- 8 human years = 50 cat years
- 12 human years = 70 cat years
- 14 human years = 80 cat years
- 16 human years = 84 cat years

By these calculations, she is a dowager in the eighth decade of her life.

Getting along…

For years, the hallmark of our relationship was a predictable early morning and late evening ritual.

At the start of the day…the start of her day…she would slip silently along the rug covered bedroom floor, hop to the bed, climb on my back where, through the cobwebs of transitioning from sleep to wake, I sensed an additional 10 pounds parked between my shoulder blades…her energetic purring like a small vibrator.

"Hey You. Here I am…let's get this day started!"

As I flipped from tummy to back, she with the aplomb of a lumbar jack in a log rolling competition expertly stayed on top. There we rested for a few minutes…two souls meditating in the mindlessness of the early morning as our – well my – engines began to increase their revolutions in preparation for the start of the day. Certain I was awake, and her 'ear scratching and back rubbing' cup full, off she hopped in anticipation of breakfast, normally at the hand of my human partner Molly.

At night, as I slipped into bed to read, do crossword puzzles or whatever, this little figure would suddenly appear beside me, climb to my chest and purr away for a few more minutes of quality time.

As she looked at me, I could imagine her saying. "It's nice to be here isn't it - a good day for me, how about you?"

Once in awhile she might climb into my lap while I watched TV, but most of our quality time opened and closed the day…this was our time.

Time and gravity…

The last couple of years, her routine has changed. She still comes to bed early in the morning. No hopping up these days, but a slow and deliberate climb up the four steps by my side of the bed, where she rather indelicately steps on and over me on her way to Molly. There she perches, rests and purrs as though the years have meant nothing. She doesn't come to me at night any more at all.

A curious thing, however, has emerged in our relationship. Since I now work out of our home, I find Leah hanging around more and in different ways. After getting coffee and heading to the back yard as the sun greets the morning sky, she limps out the door just to be with me as I sip away and read.

When watching TV for the news or some program of interest, she comes to me. This is not intermittent, from time to time; this is every time I sit for a few moments. If I don't pick her up (I mentioned there is little hopping left in those rear end springs), she softly scratches the side of my leg and stares as if to say in clever alliteration,

"I am looking for a little lap loving…you had BETTER pick me up!"

If I take an afternoon nap, no matter where she is hiding in the house, I hear the uneven pitter patter of feet (no rugs on the bedroom floor of our Tucson home), the now familiar 'up the steps' hobble as two eyes emerge at the side of the bed, pausing as if asking permission and then slipping to my chest we drift away together for a few unconscious moments….

"This is kinda nice isn't it?" her calming purrs suggests.

The workday has become the most notable to me. I spend a lot of hours behind the computer, and as I sit typing or reading, I feel a gentle rubbing on the side of my leg. Pushing back my chair, there she sits looking for a little company. When I pick her up and place her beside me on the desk she turns and wiggles, then she lies beside my arm, falls asleep with an apparent sense of contentment I cannot find words to describe.

"Yeah, this is good…just you and me working away Zzzzzzzz…"

The consequence of this is that we spend much more time together than in the past. In some regards, I began to feel she was becoming really needy…

Recently, a realization, real or imagined, slipped into my consciousness. While I don't know what or how she thinks, the sense I get is that she is saying to me in her own way…

"Listen here, my friend, my time is much shorter than yours, and I won't be here too terribly much longer. I want there to be NO QUESTION as to how much I love and have loved you in my life. My intention is to give you as much of myself as I possibly can while I am still here…. "

Today is all there is for any of us, but there is little doubt when that little creature's time is done, my heart will appreciate every gentle touch and every single purr….

YESTERDAY AND TODAY

Life is God's novel.
Let him write it!
- Isaac Singer, Author

"Ni Hao," I said when he glanced at me across the room.

"Ni Hao Ma?" he responded.

"Wo hen hao," I answered, and we both smiled.

The twinkle in his eye acknowledged my gesture of respect and awareness that I had all but exhausted the extent of my Mandarin vocabulary!

Dinner at the Hunan….
The waitress took my order and my mind drifted to Charlie. It had been a long time since I had eaten there and I wondered….wondered whether I might see him…wondered if he still worked…wondered if he was alive…

Out of the corner of the eye a familiar movement caught my attention. Emerging from the kitchen, head slightly down, he moved quietly to a table, food in hand. I watched him work as I had so many times before. His gentle and unassuming manner that had drawn my attention so many years before, warmed my heart once more as he slipped into the room.

When he was finished with his customers, he came over, and as if we had seen one another the week before, we fell into pleasantly rhythmic small talk with the refreshment of a warm shower on an early summer's morning...the hard drives of our minds returning to the sentence we had been writing the last time we had seen one another eight years earlier.

He – we – looked older, but 'felt' exactly the same as the uncounted number of times we interacted over the 25 years we had known one another.

How this happened...
I had returned to Missouri for a one-day event...a wedding I had promised I would attend.

My friend Keena, an actress from Los Angeles, was from Jefferson City. We met at a Starbucks in Hollywood on a warm fall afternoon in 2010. When this young woman approached the outdoor table where I sipped a cappuccino, I knew her instantly.

The recognition came honestly, for I had known, worked for and admired her mother for many years. In fact, I had met Keena several times decades earlier. Theressa was my department chairman when I taught at Lincoln University. A former dancer for the Harlem Ballet, she had moved on to an academic career. Having not lost her love for the craft, however, she formed and led a wonderful dance troupe at the university.

Keena....a little girl at the time...played with toys on the floor of her mother's office while the young men and women rehearsed. Occasionally, I watched these amazing young people preparing and this little girl at play.

There was no doubt, after the first five minutes at that Starbucks, this young woman and I were going to be friends...and friends we became.

It got better...
Over the next few years, while living in San Diego, Keena came down from L.A. for one reason or another. Somewhere around the time she shot a film in San Diego (A 2013 Los Angeles subway thriller called 'Red Line') I met Ajamu, her boyfriend.

Keena also produces and puts on shows – one woman and other ensembles. Every time a new project came, she invited me to come, but each time some work conflict got in the way. I did, however, follow with delight her performances on YouTube.

When it appeared she and Ajamu were serious, I told her I would do my very best to come to her wedding no matter what.

"No matter what" happened Saturday, May 2nd at La Maison event center near Jefferson City, and it was a glorious affair. The nuptials were performed outside and the day could not have appeared with more splendor. Thressa and Kenny, beautiful and handsome, were radiant with parental pride, as were Mr. and Mrs. Frazier, Ajamu's parents. I arrived at the site an hour or so early, watched with bursting heart, and after a few hugs and kisses after the ceremony, headed for St. Louis a satisfied and contented fellow.

It was, by now, nearly 6PM (the wedding getting a bit of a late start by 4:30 or so) and I was hungry. Keena had, with the directness and enthusiasm of her mother, invited me to stay for the dinner, but I knew the drive back would get me into St. Louis after dark, and said I should really head out.

Maybe because I was on automatic pilot heading into Jefferson City, I took an exit as if I were going to our old home on Kansas Street…maybe because I was thinking about what an amazing couple Keena and Ajamu were…maybe because I was supposed to be there, I found myself on Missouri Blvd., passing the Hunan Restaurant…maybe a bowl of hot and sour soup would fill the bill. I pulled in the small parking lot.

I was tired, thinking about the drive east, getting to the airport hotel and a good night's sleep, before an early morning flight home…it was one of those things that just happens.

So in I went, and there he was, my old friend Charlie!

It was a brief stop and then back on the road; my cup re-energized and overflowing from the day.

Blessing big and small…
The New York Times does a series called: "36 hours in <name the city>" providing folks on short and busy schedules, memorable things they might see or do.

My 36 hours in Missouri were more than memorable.

As I tucked in to the hotel that night, and for the final few moments of consciousness left in the day, I wondered at events that have gifted my life. As I felt myself drift away into the Netherlands of sleep, I felt the touch from the hand of God reminding me of yesterday's blessings and the wonder of those yet to come...

IN ANTICIPATION OF A LIFE

It is our duty, my young friends to resist old age,
to fight against it as we would fight against a
disease; to adopt a regimin of health;
to practice moderate exercise; and
to take just enough of food and
drink to restore our strength
and not over burden it.
- Cicero – <u>On Old Age</u>

To: Baby Robertson on his/her arrival on planet earth.

From: Uncle Ted

My dear 'BR,'

I awoke in the night thinking about you and wondering just what you might look like when you make your appearance. I suppose I should clarify that a little, because I have little doubt you will look like most babies at birth…wet, wrinkled…a little noise maker leaving the warmth of a loving and caring mother's tummy, to the harsh glare of…of, well something unknown!

Actually, you were due today, and having communicated with your mum, you seem pretty active, BUT not quite ready to emerge. I suppose, I don't blame you. When you have been living in an apparently secure place, why would you want to change addresses?

Ah, my not yet born infant friend, you will, however, find that everything about life is change. In the early days and months, it won't really matter because the things that enter your world will be so confusingly new, there won't be time to consider what you see and hear and touch and smell and taste. In fact, it will be everything you can do to just remain in the moment.

As I lay in bed, on the cusp of my 68th year, I wondered how we might interact.

When we meet, I also will be wrinkled, but much bigger and with a little less energy than you possess. You will, of course, only know me as an elderly, tired looking fellow identified as…hmmm…'uncle Ted?'…'Ted'…possibly some other family centric moniker.

Whatever the label, I am certain we – you and I – will find an identifier for the mind and the heart, and once things slow down for you, will become good friends. After all, I have a pretty good relationship with your mother, as I had with hers (my sister) and gratefully with my own.

The women in our family have been and are extraordinary human beings who brought special lights to all with whom they came in contact.

If you turn out to be a girl, I have NO DOUBT you will carry on the tradition as long as you travel into the great unknown to which you have been called. You will be taught the importance of faith in God and the values of integrity and purpose. Your mother will tell you there is NOTHING you cannot do, and with belief in that principle, you will not be restricted by thoughts of self-doubt and fear.

If, on the other hand, you are a boy, well, all I can say is that you will be the luckiest of little boys and young men. Your mother will take the time, as did mine, to teach you to respect the women and men with whom you come in contact – especially the women. I say this, because my life has been so greatly enriched by those smart and strong females whom I have just mentioned to you. Your Mum will tell you the truth…she will not pull punches and all of that will make you a better man and human being.

To be honest, at this stage of the game, I am not leaning either way and am kind of tickled not to know what gender you are. It adds some spice to the equation and in many ways it makes the entrance you will make just a little more exciting!

I only know this…hang on to your hat…you are in for the 'ride of your life'…literally!

- ted…or whatever you decide to call me!

A NEW BEGINNING

> "Only mothers can think of future, because
> they give birth to it in their children"
> Maxim Gorky – Russian writer

"Your phone is buzzing."

"Yeah, I know," I replied. "Probably some headline from the BBC."

A single buzz when my phone is on silence is usually a headline pushed from the British Broadcasting Corporation's service.

The day began...

It was unusual to still be in bed after 5AM in our time zone, but I was awake and thinking about Mariah, Dan and baby Robertson. By now the little creature was eight days late, and from the chat I had with Mariah the day before, the little character was just hanging out, with no apparent urgency to get into birth position.

Mariah and Dan are both doctors, and fully aware of the steps necessary if the baby were to get too big by staying in its current home too long: drug induced labor and/or caesarian birth...steps they had worked hard to avoid. By yesterday their physician indicated this baby was probably NOT going to emerge naturally and would need either chemical or mechanical help (surgery) to bring it to its first lung filled non-fluid breath – not particularly reassuring.

It was, as this organic life emergence ritual is for all new parents, stressful for both of them.

Getting in the game...

I was, in fact already preparing a second letter to the baby suggesting it might not be a bad idea to, as my grandmother was so fond of saying, "Get a move on!!"

This morning, Molly started the coffee as I lay there praying the baby would feel the ancient and primal urge to slip into position and descend to a world "...where no man [this baby] had gone before."

Molly burst into the bedroom and said, "Check your text messages."

It turns out the buzz was NOT the BBC, but the MLR (Mariah Lynn Robertson).

The text: "My water broke at 5:30am this morning. Ted your letter to BR worked."

In that moment I appreciated 'intention is everything,' as I had not written a word yet.

It looked like baby Robertson had sensed the prayers and cosmic messages – from many folk, I might add – and decided it was time!

The process...

Around 1PM they headed to the hospital for the final stages of the impending event.

Not having personal experience, there is a lot that goes on as the birthing event approaches. Mariah and Dan have a lot of family and friends who, during the whole pregnancy, were updated and/or in contact with them. They would all want to know details as the focal point of the process was now at hand.

I texted Dan: "We will remain 'radio silent' until we hear from you."

The day and evening passed with no news, so with the two of them – well the three of them – firmly in mind, I tucked into bed at my usual hour.

2AM – the phone buzzed! Almost instantly alert I grabbed the phone: It was the BBC, a volcano in Chile.

After calming down, I drifted back to sleep.

3:10AM – the phone buzzed! As before, it seemed that all my senses were 'ready to go: It was the BBC, an earthquake in Tibet.

5:30AM – the phone buzzed! It was the D-A-N! It was a 22.5" (57.3cm), 9lb 2oz (4.14kg) baby boy! Coen Arnott had made his appearance some 24 hours after Mariah's initial text the morning before.

Mother and baby were healthy and well – as, now were Molly and I!

Perspective – is there any?...

I have recently been reading Carl Sagan, the astrophysicist and cosmologist, whose television specials brought the science of the universe into so many of our homes in the 1990s.

I have come to appreciate there may be billions of universes, of which our planet is nothing more than a speck of dust. I appreciate billions of children have been brought to life on this 'speck of dust.' I further appreciate this primal rhythm happens in ALL species as the reproductive miracle of sustained life is invoked innumerable times every single day.

This day, however, I was cloaked with the provincial sense that none of this mattered as this drama unfolded. This day, there were no universes, no specks of dust, no billions of births in every living species we know…No, this day I could only see two young people closing the chapter that was, for them, as unique and truly unknown, as the result of the care and love that had brought all of this to bare.

This day, there was only one universe…one world…one speck of dust to me: Coen Arnott Robertson!

THE WOMB OF SELF-CONTENT

"Travel is fatal to prejudice, bigotry and narrow mindedness,
and many of our people need it sorely on these accounts…"
Samuel L. Clemens, The innocents Abroad

His name is Sam and that is about as good a place to start as any.

There were a lot of them over the years - youngsters, who seemed to have unlimited promise, and others who appeared to be quite content to be…well, just to be.

Most of the kids were compliant, making the work fairly easy and there were a few, from time to time , who seemed to always find mischief hiding around a corner or two, causing our work to be a little more challenging.

"LP" was my partner – the 'L' standing for 'Lloyann' and the 'P' her last name – and for more than two decades, we were a team, managing a church youth group.

During those years, we spent a fair number of nights camping out – complete with adolescent nocturnal sounds…days riding roller coasters or canoe floating on rivers…evenings enjoying outdoor Broadway musical theatre and a ton of time just trying to keep track of everyone. 'Elp' (nickname for my partner) was short and I tall, so I would generally take the lead in a crowd so the kids could see me, and she followed like a mother hen squiring any 'chicks' that slipped away from the group.

Sam was one of those kids.

He was a bright-eyed four-year old when we met. A quiet youngster with an alert set of eyes that always seemed to be looking for something different…something more. I was drawn to him, because optimism seemed to drift off him like gentle smoke from the embers of a campfire just right for hot dogs or chocolate, marshmallow and graham cracker s'mores. I never heard him complain, be argumentative or disruptive… he was just different ,with a twinkle in his eye suggesting he knew something you didn't.

The boy didn't draw attention to himself, but there was an undercurrent of energy that compelled a certain amount of notice, and when he was focused, there was little doubt he was completely absorbed…whether it was Pokémon with his friend Matt or earning Boy Scout merit badges that led to him becoming an Eagle Scout…you could count on his attention and intent to succeed.

The thing about this young man is that you had little doubt the trajectory of his life was going to be big – big in this case, meaning for him…by his standards. After high school, he went on to college to learn interactive digital media, worked for some time designing video games, traveled around the Western U.S., got some inspiration and headed for Korea where he taught school, traveled through Asia and honed what had become fairly formidable skills in Team Frisbee. Yes sir, Team Frisbee…a young man in flight! The game at which he became so skilled was a great metaphor for life…his!

Over the years, I have traveled and written a travelogue that I send home every few days. When Sam was younger, I told him it would be great to travel together sometime when he had put on a few years. My real interest was to expose him to the broader world in which we live…to encourage him to widen his peripheral vision as much as possible…to let him appreciate that life is much more and much different than he might expect.

Actually, I did this with a number of the youth in my church group over the years, but whether it was my influence or not, Sam reached out and embraced the world…he has taken a position on the 'bow of the ship' in his life and felt the wind in his face…emerging from the womb of self-content…opening doors, behind which he does not know what to expect and in many ways said, "Bring it on life!"

Sam and I have written some since those early days, and when I get a personal email from him, it has always been great. The method by which I now keep up, however…his travelogue of sorts…is his Facebook page…the anonymous 'keeper upper.'

They say success is passing on the passion you feel for the things that drive you and bring satisfaction. There is little doubt many of us find great fulfillment in our work, but for me, it has been the 'things around the edges' that have brought the greatest gratification to my life…the small things…the touches from other people along the way. Traveling and meeting the 'yet unknown' brings richness to the streets and byways of the world in which I live.

Keeping tabs on Sam's life has been like watching the changing nuances of sunlight against the face of a mountain as the day progresses; there is always something new…something before unseen…that adds a new sense of appreciation in the passing of the day. While sunset is not a terribly far distance for me, Sam is in the late morning of his life…the sky is clear, the sun bright with much more to see and explore.

OLD DOGS

"If you believe old dogs cannot learn
new tricks...'YOU' never will."
– Anonymous

Heather begins by saying,

"Let's start with a gentle warm up."

"What is the most important thing to know in what we are about to do?"

By now the twenty or so folk gathered in the conference room know the answer, and with smiles all around say together, "Breathe!" And with that, the practice begins.

Strange, I never thought I would find myself doing this...

Another time, in another land...
They moved slowly in smooth rhythmic fashion, wearing loose and baggy garments; the men in plain colors; the women a little more brightly dressed, their gazes unfocused and distant. There were 30 or more of them, and from across the open area, they looked as though they were connected to one another by an invisible wire, tugged in unison by an unseen puppeteer...exotic to say the least.

It was Guangzhou, China, early morning as daylight peeked over the eastern horizon as if to see whether anything had changed since it had turned off the lights and tucked into the western edges of the skyline at the end of the previous day...not much had.

The park was full of older early morning exercisers, doing a variety of activities. On low hanging branches, a small number of men were suspended, stretching out their shoulder joints. Other folk walked slowly backward, occasionally peeking over their shoulders to ensure they were on the right track. There were one or two using a stick to push small hoops as they walked. In a small area, there was a large bumpy concrete pad upon which some folk were walking barefoot to toughen up their feet. Then there was that group of elderly men and women doing early morning Tai Chi.

As I jogged along the riverfront by the open park in a pair of shorts, tee shirt and tennis shoes, there is little doubt I was, if not quite so exotic, completely out of place. The occasional person tapped their neighbor, pointing my way as if they had seen a large, pale skinned alien from outer space. I heard, "Gwai Lo," (pronounced Qu-eye low) a word meaning 'foreigner,' drift through the air a time or two.

I was impressed so many people seemed to make this part of their morning routine. On subsequent mornings when exercising in other parts of the country I saw this again and again. Nobody was dressed in spandex or the latest gym attire. I didn't see fashionable shoes or slick looking headbands. It was just folk dressed in comfortable clothing getting ready for the day.

Education, a barrier to entry…

My professional career has been in the area of counseling, testing, treating and designing exercise programs for clinical populations. Over the years, these have included: spinal cord injured, cardiac, pulmonary, arthritic, and for the last two and a half decades, people with chronic back and neck pain. There are a lot of things that can be done to help improve functional activity levels when people find themselves trapped in the cobweb of chronic disease, but for me Tai Chi was certainly NOT one of them.

Watching these folk practicing Tai Chi in China was interesting and fun, but in my world it wasn't really exercise, as I had been trained…it was just a curiosity.

It goes like this…

When I was a graduate student, I knew everything and was certain if the people listened to me, their health and lives would be much improved. With the zeal of a young Pentecostal evangelist armed with scripture, and little life experience, my ignorant confidence was as solid as the rock of Gibraltar.

I didn't know, in those years, I had contracted a toxic and potentially lethal disease. It is a virus one picks up in graduate school, and, if they manage to stay out of the real world, it can develop into full-blown CAA – *Chronic Academic Arrogance*. This is an illness that emerges in many professions – sometimes referred to as the 'plague of the self-right,' but institutions of higher learning, in particular, provide a petri dish in which this infection thrives. Complicating matters, the victims almost never know they are a carrier, and as a result actually believe they are well!

It turns out this horrible disease is really hard to eradicate. Remission does happen, and when it does, the carrier's quality of life is much better, but there is always the danger of a relapse that can, as one ages, make their lives miserable.

A few things are helpful in fighting the illness…life experience and failure. There is one other thing, and that is aging! I suppose aging encompasses the previous two, but sometimes the disorder is so profound, one does not learn either from experience or failure!!

Life is change…

The thing about getting older is that stuff just doesn't work as well as it did in years gone by. I have found, as everyone who has preceded me in the unavoidable reduction of life force, I can't run as fast…jump as high…remember specific things as easily…hear and see quite so clearly. That is not to say, I'm ready to cash in the chips, it is simply to say, like those old nickel cadmium batteries, my energy levels never seem to fully recharge!

This unavoidable phenomenon, brings with it a whole series of questions that were not on the table in earlier years, and as I have found myself 'climbing the rope' in certain aspects of my life, things I recommended for people when I was NOT '*on the rope*,' do not work as well as I had once imagined. I have come to appreciate that if I had to take all of the advice I have given in my life, things might not have worked out so well for me.

Things that are important now have everything to do with creating and/or maintaining the best quality of life I can – this encompasses care in the areas of food, sleep, activities that help to calm my mind and regular exercise.

This brings me back to Heather…Heather, my Tai Chi teacher. What I once thought was just an 'Eastern curiosity,' and/or something done by people who lived in California, has had a real and meaningful impact on my life.

The evidence…

One of the things I have noticed in recent years is a small incremental change in balance. I knew that lifting weights and/or doing Tai Chi had been demonstrated in research to be helpful. When I first noticed the balance issue, I adjusted my lower extremity strengthening routine and it helped. It seemed, however, that I got all the benefit from strengthening that I could, so I decided to try Tai Chi…something I would NEVER have done earlier in my life.

I have been amazed at the results in a short period of time. A small example, and this may be too much information... Putting on trousers while standing recently required a bit of hopping around to keep balanced while slipping each leg in. After a month and a half of weekly meetings and a little 'practice' at home, the ease with which I put them on was just short of amazing. I would never have predicted such a rapid result.

Getting older has its challenges, but it also has its benefits. Some of the barriers to learning, created by 'CAA,' of necessity slip away, melting into the reality of changing interests and needs, and that is a good thing. Embracing the changes has enhanced my quality of life.

So, "What is the most important thing to know in what we are about to do?"

(say this with a smile)

"Breathe…."

AN OLD YELLOW VAN

"Heaven goes by favor. If it went by merit, you
would stay out and your dog would go in."
- Mark Twain

The yellow 1967 yellow Ford Econoline pickup truck, sat in the parking lot at the YMCA.

It shone brightly in the morning sun as if to say, "Hey, you…do I look familiar?"

As the guy got out of the truck, I said, "I used to drive one of those, but it was an OD (Olive Drab) green military van."

He smiled and said, "I'd sell her if I could! Are you interested?"

I returned an "I don't think so" grin, but, nonetheless, there were fond memories of a bygone era when bumping and shaking along the country roads of rural Alabama to the smell of fresh growing peanuts, corn, an anticipation of watermelon season, and a more than faint odor of motor oil burning from an engine that sat between the front seats. If you had a military license in those days, it was almost a rite of passage!

If you want to wake up your taste buds and satisfy your soul, put a watermelon or two in the refrigerator, give them a day to chill and then eat your heart out as you bury your face in the refreshing, chilled heart of the melon! There is little on a hot and humid Southern Alabama day that calms the angry beast, more than ice-cold watermelon!

46

Memory is a funny thing. As the sharp edges have softened with the river of time, the feelings they generated have not. In fact, in some ways they seem to intensify, and I can say with authoritative assurance that the memory of cold watermelon on a hot summer's day is richer than the sweet lips of the first girl ever I kissed!

Fort Rucker, Alabama…

It was 1970, and even though this vehicle had more than six-figures worth of 'military abusive driving mileage' under its belt, there was still a little life in it. The shocks were so bad, and the seats so well worn, that every bump and rough spot in the road could be felt as it made its daily runs to our radar site in Headland, Alabama.

This van had a standard transmission and required a practiced touch to make it shift smoothly. "Shift smoothly…" might be an over exaggeration, but anyone who has military van driving experience, knows exactly what I mean!

The engine was in the center of the vehicle between the driver and front seat passenger and was covered with an insulated metal shell that was supposed to dampen the sound and keep the heat from filling the van. The center console engine might not have had the greatest admiration from mechanics, but you could put almost anything on that thing from notebooks to take out lunch for the driver and passengers – front and back.

Yes indeed, driving or riding in those old vans, was an experience not to be lost to the foggy back roads of memory.

The memory two-edged…

The puppy lay softly whimpering, on the center console this cool spring morning, as I headed to the veterinarian's office in town…the engine warming his little body…my heart in my throat.

"I am so sorry," I said as the little creature looked up at me.

It had been a valiant effort. Jim had wanted to kill the pup as soon as he realized there was a problem.

"No," I said. I had been going over to his place every morning to play with it in the two months since it's birth.

"I'll take him to the Vet in town and get him taken care of." I said. "I'll take care of the bills."

"Suit yo self," Jim said. "Ain't nothin' no vet gonna do for the mange. That pup done already been dead!"

Radar neighbor across the road…
Jim was a day laborer on the outskirts of Headland, Alabama, working just for wages and no stock in the land or its crops. He was in his late 70s and lived in a single room house with his wife, Anna, across the road from the radar site where I worked.

Sometimes in the late afternoons when we waited for the night flight helicopters to come and practice radar approaches to our 'cow pasture runway,' I would head over to Jim's and sit on his tiny porch, where he would tell me stories about what it was like to live in the segregated South.

"Anna be walkin' back from town, and sometime thos white boys throwed bottles at her…called her names."

"One night, back in '42, the Klan come in the middle of the night and took one of my boys," he said. "They didn't kill him, but hurt him bad."

The puppy…
Jim and Anna had a female mongrel dog, who had a litter that year. It took too much to care for them, and he said he gave some away to his boys. I think he drowned the rest…. but he let me have one with the promise I would feed it and take care of it.

"This puppy does have the mange," said the Veterinarian, confirming Jim's diagnosis.

"We can try to treat the skin lesions, but this kind is a problem and the treatment may not help."

"Is there a chance?" I said.

"Slim," he replied

"Let's try," I said, and we did.

After a month I took the pup to, the Vet.

"Treatment's not working. It's time."

"Give me one more day?"

"Yeah," he replied

I spent the rest of the day with that little thing and the next morning, before taking him in. I played with him, rubbed his belly, talked as sweet as I knew how and fed him good.

Only one of us knew this would be our last time, and this his last meal. I tried to slow the time down – tried to make it stop…but couldn't do it, and here we were on the "…last ride."

The vet asked me if I wanted to stay, or wanted the body. I told him I couldn't bear it and could he take care of the body.

I nuzzled that pup, said good bye, walked out to that OD green van and cried all the way back to the radar site.

Here and now...
My mind jumped back in that instant from that OD green…to the bright yellow Econoline in the parking lot.

The fella said, "I'd sell her if I could! Are you interested?

I returned an "I don't think so grin," and headed into the YMCA for my morning workout, and the lightening memory of a little pup that had touched my heart so many years ago….

HEY! HOW DID <u>YOU</u> GET HERE?

> "So far so good. Give me a little more
> life and I'll write the report…"
> - Anonymous

It's a miracle I am alive, I thought.

How did this happen? I wondered…

Hmmm…I am not exactly sure! Maybe I don't need to know all the details, but there are a few things I understand.

Pondering a little…

We often use the expression 'miracle of life' when attempting to describe the unspeakably amazing phenomenon of birth, beginning with the primal drive to propagate our species.

A remarkable number of coordinated/complicated things must exactly align for conception to take place, so the biochemical and physiologic processes of growth can occur in the womb.

During the 'successful event,' for example, millions of sperm compete for a single egg waiting to be fertilized…each one carrying minutely different combinations of genetic material.

Under normal circumstances one, and only one gets through and conception takes place. It is so astonishing, that had a different sperm fertilized the egg, you and I might look different than we do. Now there's a cosmic '…what if??!!...'

That's just the beginning.

While gestating in the isolation of our mother's womb, the biochemical building blocks of life, following the DNA/RNA recipe, build a physical body cell by cell. No easy task considering each of us is custom made according to the specifications of a blueprint, discarded and never again used in the creation of a human body.

If we survive the process, escaping the warmth of our mother's belly – and it is quite obvious we did - we emerge into an alien, hostile and chaotic world providing the oxygen needed for our 'first breath.'

Just getting here far exceeds the possibilities of winning a lottery of any size!

It is a miracle I am alive, I thought

An aside to the unknown – the really unknown…
Somewhere along the line, 'consciousness' is injected into our little developing brains, but that is a topic exceeding the grasp of even the best and most thoughtful minds…a topic that continues to elude science and remains in the category of "…that is simply just the way it is…" Thomas Aquinas said, the things we don't understand, we put under the category of '…God's workings….'

Back it up just a little…
Consider for a moment the number of wars in the history of the world – okay, maybe we don't know the exact number, but trust me, it is a BIG number…a number that has led to millions and millions dying as cannon fodder for forgotten disagreements that ended their lives.

Consider the number of premature accidental or purposeful deaths for whatever reason…famine, disease, anger, jealousy…each one eliminating the possibilities of future offspring…each one stopping the genetic chain of events that would bring forth an inherited strain of anything!

It IS a miracle I am alive, I thought.

Consider, the obstacles for:
  - surviving childbirth,
  - escaping childhood,
  - passing through the stupidity of adolescence,

- the laissez-faire young adulthood, and/or
- the minefields of the mature years.

If you are a bit older like me, think of the traffic accidents, falls, head bangings, possible near drownings, and other potential 'life enders' we have dodged…sometimes by the skin of our teeth!

Since you are reading this, each of you has outlived the gauntlet of events, historical and/or personal, that could have prematurely ended your life!

It's a miracle WE ARE alive, I thought.

Getting to old age is a very tricky business. Crossing the finish line, of '…from dust thou are to dust thou shalt return…' relatively intact, if one might be so bold to say, is a notable feat in spite of the fact our 'suit' has become a little wrinkled in the process.

I'm just saying…

While there are millions and millions of reasons why you and I should never have been born, nor taken a single breath, nor reached any level of consciousness, here we are – me writing and you reading this piece…alive, breathing…carbon based creatures given the gift to express a complexity of experience through the sensations of sight, sound, touch, smell and taste…each one providing us opportunity for reflection, creating a whole new world of possibility with each breath.

Yeah, it is a miracle WE are alive, and in the context of so many reasons why we shouldn't be…I'm pretty grateful we are!

IT'S HARD TO STAY OUT OF THE ROOM

> "In my Father's house are
> many mansions [rooms]:
> if it were not so, I would
> have told you…"
> - John 14:2: Bible

Sometimes it is impossible to stay out of the room.

Actually, there are a lot of rooms in the house. More rooms than a fellow could possibly visit…at least not all at one time.

The reading room is a great place to spend time. There is so much to learn …things one would never experience on their own…mostly because there simply isn't time. It is voyeurism at its most meaningful – full of adventures, mysteries, histories of remarkable women and men filling them all. In the reading room, one gets the sense just how delicate and interconnected we all are.

Here we can see how the tiniest ripple in the pond of humanity can change an entire course of history. In this room, it is very easy to say, "I didn't know that!" or "So that's how that works!" It is here where one finds a whole range of emotions…out loud laughter, gentle tears, heart pounding excitement, or one's deepest fears. Yes sir, that reading room is something else.

Then there is the music room…what a great place that is. Wow! The amount of music that has gone through the walls of that place – it is unimaginable! It seems the great thing about the music room is the amazing variety of both sound and feeling that comes when listening to all of those wonderful noises – for they are, in many ways simply that…organized noises vibrating through the air (no wires here) and touching us in the deepest of places. Gospel, rock and roll, country, bluegrass, opera, symphony, folk, musical theatre, African, South American…the words, the rhythms…there is so much, it is sometimes impossible to try to recall even parts of it. The great thing about this room is not just the variety, but the way one can find exactly the right music that touches the soul…you know, custom fit – tailored just for each one of us.

I particularly like the cooking room – I mean, who doesn't? The things in that larder are almost overwhelming, what with the amazing variety and combinations of plants and animals and fish and fowl. The bounty that passes through this room is awesome. It's not just what is there, but the process of preparing it. Who could not recall the smell of warm bread in the oven or coffee brewing in the early morning hours? The comfort of having something warm on a cold winter's day, or something cold in the heat of the summer. There is such an assortment, it is difficult to imagine all the variations.

The workroom occupies a lot of time.

To do anything meaningful in the workroom, a lot of energy must be spent in the schoolroom – whether it be learning a mental or physical task. The schoolroom is a must, just to get permission to enter the workroom. There surely are lessons learned outside the formality of school, but NOTHING is accomplished without time spent formally or informally in that place, but I digress. The great thing about the workroom room is the continual sharpening of the sword that happens here. It turns out the workroom is really just the schoolroom in disguise. The more time spent here, the better skilled one becomes, and the more skilled one becomes, the more one learns…it is a marvelous cycle!

Lots of us spend time in the management room…the place where one works through the issues confronted on a daily basis. We are creatures designed to ask questions and to solve problems that pop up as we float on the river of life…you know, the unexpected swiftness of rapids…the water falls…the tree across the way…all of the unanticipated things we engage…problems we solve and issues we undertake. You see, in addition to question askers, we are problem solvers. We like nothing better than successfully solving a problem. This is how the great adventurers and conquerors of history created civilizations…spurred by questions – the 'what if' – entering the unknown. Somehow we are just wired that way –

success bringing a degree of satisfaction…failure bringing disappointment and frustration.

Then there is the distraction room. In fact, one could argue, depending how one spends their time in the variety of rooms available in our house, the distraction room may influence all the others. You know what I mean…the reading room, the music room, the cooking room, the work/school room, the management room…all of them occupying time to avoid the reality room.

Yeah – the reality room…hmmm. Sometimes this is a meaningful and helpful place. It puts things in perspective…creates a sense of objectivity…clarity. Sitting there quietly and assessing the elements of our lives often brings a little realism to our thought process. Occasionally this room needs the help of others to get it properly furnished. We don't always see things as they are (whatever that really means); so a little assistance from an outside source can be helpful.

I have avoided talking about the family room. This room can be complicated…very complicated. You pick your friends, but you are born into your family. Gratefully, this has been a great room in my life, providing the foundation materials for all the other rooms of my house. It set the context…focused the view…created the basic template. Even with the loss of my parents, it has remained strong and solid. This room has a lot of smaller rooms, and one of those smaller rooms is, at this time of my life, the most painful…the 'sister room.'

The past couple of years, I've been spending as much time as possible in the rooms mentioned here, and many more, it might be added. All of them, however have been colored by the 'distraction room' to avoid the 'reality room,' but mostly to keep out of the 'sister room.'

The sister room was always my favorite. It was a secure room…a place of comfort…a known commodity. It was such a familiar room; it was easy to simply take it for granted. Even being the single male with two sisters, it has been a great room full of so many meaningful experiences.

But now as my sister's health and mind deteriorate at an astounding pace, it is a fearful and frustrating place. It is a room where knowledge fails me…where the music plays only chaotic dissonance…the food left a little too long on the counter…the work meaningless and the management…well, the management seems nothing more than a series of diminishing efforts in a losing battle. No solution to the problem, no gratification for success...simply the emptiness of the unavoidable conclusion.

For the most part, I stay out of this room...but there are the moments in the quiet of the night when it seems all the rooms I so love, are locked up tight, and I am driven to the 'sister room.' It is here where the remembered laughter and joy turns to tears...it is here where the '...tigers come...' to tear at the fabric of memory.

And yet, it is in these quiet moments of despair, when I am unable to keep from sinking into the quagmire of self pity, she comes to me with all the vibrancy and strength that was her life...she comes with the quickness of wit and the quietness we often shared just being together. She draws me into the memory room, pulling me from the darkness, reminding me there is a context...there is a meaning, even if for the moment it is unknown. In this room, the air is filled with the knowledge of a lifetime of experience, the aroma of love, the music of faith, and the hope of the yet unseen.

Of all the rooms God has created in the house that is my mind...it is here in my memories where I find solace for my soul.

THE EARLY MORNING HOURS

> "I think we dream so we don't have to be apart so long.
> If we're in each other's dreams, we can
> be together all the time."
> - Bill Watterson,
> Calvin & Hobbs

It was…as usual…GREAT to see her.

Through many of our years we have been close to one another and for many years as children and adults, lived in the same house. There were periods of time when we were separated by school or work, but even then we never failed to find some of the one-on-one time we treasured.

Same family, same name…
As youngsters we didn't much value family. You know the kind of thing that happens. You grow up in the same house and that is pretty much your entire world.

In the beginning, you come to the planet '…first come first serve…' For some reason, life doesn't take dinner reservations. In fact, when you come to the party, there is no way to know who will even be there!

When I arrived, there was already a 'place holder' in the family unit. My older sister, Anne, had made her entrance two years earlier, and I soon discovered she was the life of the party. At first I didn't even realize she was there, but slowly it became apparent someone other than me was getting attention in the space I had come to occupy.

Wait...what about me?

A short two years later, I found myself in the same position as my older sister, when Nancy appeared on the scene. Quite unexpectedly, one day in May, mother went away for a few days. She returned with another little person in tow. Who invited this person to the dance?? I mean, for two years it had been a struggle getting the kind of attention I wanted in the presence of a more mature and experienced sibling.

It's hard to say exactly what my older sister felt when suddenly the singular attention she had been receiving turned in to a 50/50 profit sharing deal – I do know what I felt when it became 33/33/33. My stock had been diluted without a moment's consultation on the part of my parents...mildly free floating anxiety describing it best. I mean, what if the shares got further diluted to say 25% or 20%?

Time...what a deal!

As the years passed, this rivalry for attention seemed to shift from:
"Hey, what about me?" to
"Hey, what are you up to?" to
"Hey, you are kind of interesting," to
"Hey, what's been going on in your life?" to
"Hey, I'm looking forward to seeing you on the holiday," to
"Hey, you have no idea how much I love you!"

And here she was once again. All Nancy had to do was get out of the car, walk in the room, turn on the smile, slip her arms around me and all was right with the world. She has the gift you know...the kind that no amount of childhood rivalry or seeking for attention can overcome. Two things happen every time I see her, without her speaking a word. I feel a sense of assurance, and for some totally unknown reason, a sense of confidence that whatever has been challenging, in whatever moment, can be overcome.

Family – a team sport...

It was like this today. She had been gone on business for a while and was coming home. If you ever played a team sport you will understand the relationship I have with my sister.

At first, in any game, the key is to learn the fundamentals. This is a totally self-focused task – learn to dribble the ball...run drills...do certain plays from the recipe book...try not to look silly. Then the game begins. Early in the process, many mistakes are made...passes dropped...shots missed...other players not being where they are supposed to be.

Once the fundamentals become part of the skill set – winning is the goal! Mistakes aside - winning is what it is all about isn't it? The attention goes to the winner! What could be better than that??

If you are fortunate to play the game long enough, however, something magical begins to happen. Without realizing it, you know where the other players are almost by instinct…dribbling, passing, shooting…all of that, become simply vehicles for a more mature experience…the experience of love – love of the game. No, that's not right…a yearning and love for the integrated play with others as if you were one body, one spirit…simply 'one.' There is power in that kind of 'one.' Reminiscent of Christ's prayer in the garden near the end of his life "…make them one, as you and I are one…"

My relationship with Nancy is like that. So when she came by last night it was all of the above and more. The 'knowing' as it has been for decades…the unspoken feeling we share with one another from a game we have nurtured and grown and understand so well.

A dinner date…

We had some pizza, but that was only an excuse. Pizza…geeze, we both have an unnatural capacity for the stuff. I try to keep away from it because I like it so much…I have almost no control – nor does she. We have this addiction, so it's usually best to simply stay out of the danger zone – the pizza parlor! Last night, we bit the bullet and ate our hearts out!

She brought me up to date on a couple of her projects. I told her I was trying to write some, but it wasn't easy. Somehow, I just didn't have the words to express the things I felt. She looked over the table and said what she often did, "You can do it kiddo. Just keep at it. You know the drill in life, it's just one foot in front of the other." We laughed a little and shared another story or two, catching up on people we both knew.

She was telling me about one of the guys at work that had been giving her a hard time. This narrative has been part of our family dialogue for all of my life…the difficulty women have…in particular the issues professional women often face, to which men seem oblivious and frequently promote. With only a little irritation, she always filled me in on the '…girl's perspective…'

Something was wrong…

She was just getting to the point of her story, when I felt a little disoriented. I wondered for a second whether something in the pizza had disagreed with me. I tried to focus on her conversation, but felt the room slipping away…I tried to get up, but couldn't. Someone was tapping me on the shoulder as I fought to stay alert - "…no, no wait a minute…"

Through the mist that accompanies the moments of moving from sleep to awake, I realized it had been a dream. How could it have been, it was so real…I tried to get back to the pizza parlor to no avail….the 'person' tapping me on the shoulder was Leah, one of our cats, reminding me of our morning ritual. Was she the dream and Nancy the reality? I love that cat, but damn – the morning had come.

REM sleep is the part of the cycle that ushers us in and out of the deep sleep necessary for undistracted maintenance and healing to take place in our bodies. It is the time, going in and coming out, where the dream world fills us with possibilities. It is a place where the strangest of circumstances seem to be absolutely real, with an odd sort of order. There have been only a few times, when my dreams have been so reality based…where waking has appeared to be the illusion.

Last night was one such dream. I have little doubt this night vision could be explored for deep-rooted psychological analysis, but I have little interest in that. Waking to the reality of Nancy's devastating illness was like finding myself in a bare room, in a small building in the middle of a bleak desert.

There is just a little more…
Dreams have a way of healing sometimes, or at the very least, help bring vibrancy to moments that are otherwise unwelcome and overwhelming. In moments like this, I tell her quietly in my heart, that I am trying to cope, but don't have the words to express the way I feel.

I sense her looking over the table and saying what she so often did, "You can do it kiddo. Just keep at it. You know the drill in life, it's just one foot…"

CLOSING THE LOOP

"Two possibilities exist: either we are alone in the
Universe or we are not. Both equally terrifying."
- Arthur C. Clarke

Tucson is not a place you "...get to from here..." so, usually, homeward
bound flights change either in Dallas or Chicago – it was Dallas this time on
my way home from New Jersey.

I had just settled into 20B when a voice said, "I think I'm by the
window." I smiled and said, "Well then, I guess this row is done," and
slipped into the aisle as he took his seat.

I have a small verbal toolkit to determine whether I will engage my
seatmate on flights. Marcus Aurelius says that if you have a choice between
working, or interacting with another human being, you should engage the
latter, so I look for opportunities to see what is going on in my fellow
passenger's minds.

The questions...
Usually I gently probe with a something like:

"Are you heading out or going home?"

If heading home: "Where are you coming in from?"
If heading out: "Where are you headed?"

Two or three follow ups related to what kind of work they do; how they got started in their job; did they enjoy the time with (or looking forward to seeing) their family/etc., and I can tell quickly whether I am going to be chatting or working for the rest of the flight.

The chat…

After the '…seatbelt/oxygen mask/nearest exit/read the card in the seatback pocket…' announcements were finished, I wondered whether this fellow would be interested in a conversation. Not the totally dullest tack in the box, I picked up on his accent immediately and said,

"What the heck is a Brit doing going to Tucson?"

In this case, it was the only question necessary to get the conversation going.

Andrew was a compact man, in his fifties, wearing non descript greyish clothing that was casual and comfortable looking. He had spent 25 years in British Intelligence before joining the IT security team of a well known international company, and was heading to Tucson for an annual meeting with an elite group of colleagues – game on!

As I expected, he didn't/couldn't talk specifics regarding his work, but was very engaging in the broader brush strokes of his profession. He had worked to monitor emerging issues in the Middle East and among other things, had thoughts regarding how to defang some of the extremist, terrorist threats in which the West has found itself entangled.

He had been fascinated with computers from a youngster, and began talking to me about one of his hero's Alan Turing. He shared how Turing's efforts to develop the first rudimentary mechanical device (not rudimentary at the time) had unlocked Nazi Germany's 'enigma' code. It was that successful effort permitting the Allies to win World War II.

Being a deeply informed individual, I said,

"Yeah, I really enjoyed the <u>Imitation Game</u> too. I saw it a couple of weeks ago!"

With the subtlest of questioning looks, he indicated he didn't know of the movie, he was simply a fan of Turing! It was a little hard to recover from the shallowness of my 'Turing knowledge,' but I said, a little lamely, the movie was great and that Benedict Cumbarbatch had given a spectacular performance.

"I'll make a point to see the film when it comes to England," he said.

"By the way," he continued, "there is a film called 'Castles in the Sky' you might be interested in seeing too. It is the story of Robert Watson-Watt, who invented radar, saving Britain from being completely devastated by Nazi bombing in the Second World War. It sounds like a historical parallel to the Turing movie."

I wrote it down!

The afterglow…

When I got home, I looked for the film and found it was NOT available with American 'on demand' services. Broadcast in September of 2014, it was a 'BBC Two' production not yet in release here. I had given it a good effort, but it became clear I was not going to see that film anytime soon…no big deal.

Nice flight, engaging conversation – done. Next?

The 'loop' from this chat would not close for more than a month.

Recently overseas…

Several months later, I was in Denmark on business and came home through London. I had a meeting there, so I stayed two nights with friends.

Spending time with people you know is SO MUCH BETTER than tucking into a sterile hotel room somewhere. You merge, ever so briefly, into their lifestyle, and because it was the end of the weekend…the lifestyle was relaxed.

Sunday evening, we watched episodes one and two of the first season of the BBC's Sherlock Holmes, starring Benedict Cumbarbatch. After seeing these, I was even more impressed with the actor.

Then, in a moment of inspiration, I asked whether we might find and watch 'Castles in the Sky.' As it turned out, they had premium services, but NOT BBC Two…Oh well, not so big a deal. I tucked it away for future reference.

Monday as fate would have it, my meeting was in a part of London near the Sherlock Holmes' Museum. I didn't realize it until I put together the route (train and underground) taking me to Oxford-Circus station where I would meet a colleague. Heading into the city early, so as to be sure I would know exactly where I was going, there was time to walk the few blocks to the museum.

I thought,
This is great! I just watched the Sherlock films last night and by chance, 221B Baker Street is close enough to visit!

I found the Museum and the famous address with little trouble.

I love it when unexpected things like this happen! They provide subtle shades of color to the tapestry of my life…a lovely experience. Next?

Heading home…

Tuesday morning, it was off to Heathrow…home to Tucson and my own bed! When I return home from a trip, there is little more inviting than slipping between familiar sheets and drifting into the nocturnal netherworld of comfort and Technicolor dreams!

I had some work for the trip, but it was 10 hours from London to Dallas so there would be time to nap, read or watch a film. Chasing the sun (heading west), by the way, means the entire flight is in the daylight. Somehow that seems to reduce jet lag – at least for me.

After a couple of hours and dinner, a film seemed like a good idea, but as is often the case, there wasn't anything interesting. The 'new releases' didn't catch my fancy and the available television shows were equally uninviting. I thought I would see what offerings there might be in the foreign film section. There were two films, one of which turned out to be – 'Castles in the Sky!!' *Are you kidding me!?*

It's not that this film was a burning issue for me; it wasn't really that I felt it was even important. It was that I had given my best effort to try and see it, both at home and with my friends in London. It was just that when I put the idea behind the back burner of my brain, it showed up as one of the foreign films on the flight!

Yeah, you might be saying to yourselves, "So what? – What's the big deal?"

I understand the sentiment, but that would be because you are not me.

My life has been full of these small reinforcing vignettes…so many, in fact, I have come to expect the unexpected. That is not exactly right…better said, I have come to enjoy these little presents – gifts really – from God. They constantly remind me that when I let go, accept and trust the process of the Universe to do its thing, I have the most wonderful little 'touches' that so enrich my life.

Yes sir, when those open loops close – and many of them do not…or at least I don't know they do – when those open loops close, the wonder and overwhelming magnitude of it all reminds me somebody, somewhere is watching me out of the corner of His eye…

HARDER THAN I THOUGHT

"Even when all is known, the cure of a man is not
yet complete...he must also take exercise..."
- Hippocrates: <u>Regimen</u>

Molly had been asking me with the regularity of the rising sun to come to her exercise classes. My consistent, "Thanks hon, probably not this time," responses did NOT deter her from continuing to '...drip water on the roughened pebbbles of my mind...'

Other than group yoga, which we did for two or three years in Detroit, I have avoided group exercise programs – I just don't like 'em. I bike and lift weights pretty regularly and swim a little less frequently than in the past, so I'm thinking in the delicacy of my late 60s, I'm doing plenty!

PLUS...there are all those people!!!

This last year, however, I joined the YMCA Board of Managers. Tony, our new executive director, has brought an infectious enthusiasm to an already pretty successful center.

I thought,

You know, if I am on this board, I should probably sample the classes and get a feel for the products we deliver.

After all, I'm in pretty good shape for a 'non-competitive' guy my age.

"Molly," I said. "Since I'm on the board, I'm thinking about taking a few group exercise classes. Where do you think I should begin?"

Hardly suppressing her enthusiasm at my proactive request, she suggested I try the 'Silver Sneakers Cardio' and the '50+ Boot camp' classes – it just so happens she is in both of them!

Sure, I thought, *I can do that AND kill two birds with one stone*...see what the classes are like and satisfy Molly's long standing appetite to get me into group exercise sessions. You know what they say, "Gratification delayed can be so much sweeter," and at this "...finally he's doing it..." request to her, she was feeling pretty sweet!!

Silver Sneakers...

When the studio doors opened, 30 hardy, and well past middle aged souls trickled into the room. They knew the drill – pick up the hand weights, rubber bands with handles and small 6 inch in diameter balls. My 'guide' – that would be Molly – shuttled me through the 'getting ready process' and we were ready to go.

I looked around, checking out the competition, thinking to myself,

Everyone in here, with few exceptions, is my age or older. I can do this!

The leader, Natalie, wandered to the front of the class. In my most enlightened, anti-misogynist frame of mind, I saw a 'soft around the edges' woman in her late forties to early fifties with a "I have had my kids, and this time is for me" look.

She paused for a moment, then as the energetic music started, she began exhorting the group, and for the next 50 minutes, with two or three short water breaks, it was 'Katy bar the door' non-stop activity.

When we were finished...I was DONE!! More than that, I was done and humbled at the fitness levels of these tired looking old people! Worse, Molly looked like she was just getting going.

Damn! I thought. *Tomorrow has got to be a better day!*

50s+ Boot camp...

We arrived at the door to this studio a little before 7am where there were four or so older women quietly chatting.

I noted that Shelley was there. Molly had introduced me to her before…a 59 year-old woman with a big boned body. I had seen her lifting in the weight room, and after watching her work out, there is little doubt I would want her on my team – no matter what the game might be!

Blanca our leader arrived a little before the appointed time to open the doors and get things ready. While the Silver Sneakers class is apparently the same every day, it is not so for the Boot camp. Here, the small groups of folk gather around a white dry erase board to find out what the day will bring.

We single filed through the equipment room picking up hand weights and a Bosu ball – a large ball cut in half with a hard plastic bottom and an inflated soft-topped half ball. It is used for balancing and core exercise activities.

Blanca, an animated deceptively fit woman in her fifties, headed to the front of the room, and like the day before, she paused for a moment as the energetic music began and for the next 50 minutes, with two or three short water breaks, it was, as it had been with Natalie, 'Katy bar the door' non-stop activity.

For comparative purposes, Natalie was like a Protestant minister in most mainstream churches, whereas Bianca, was the Evangelical, Pentecostal exhorter of the less than lively sheep under her early morning ministry.

Natalie had command of her class, Blanca 'owned' hers.

As she wandered around the studio she encouraged and exhorted those aging bodies.

"Come on, keep those heads up when you are doing pushups!"

"Hey, are you looking for buried treasure on the floor? If you find it let me know!"

"Woo!!"

"That's it keep going." "How does it feel?"

"If it is too much, modify your activity!"

She knew everyone's name and seemed to have a connection with every person in the room.

When it was over, I thought…

Damn!! Today was NOT better!

Worse…Molly, as the day before, seemed refreshed when we were done.

I will continue to take these classes and some others the Y offers, as part of trying to gain a better understanding what we do and how we do it. There is little doubt I will get into better shape than I am already in…or that I am NOT in…

The only problem I foresee is that Molly might find something else she thinks will benefit the quality of my life…

LAUGHING COYOTES

> "Let us toast to animal pleasures, to escapism…and to the
> 'good life,' whatever it is and wherever it happens."
> - Hunter Thompson: <u>The Proud Highway</u>:
> <u>Saga of a Desperate Southern Gentleman</u>

I live on Laughing Coyote Way in Oro Valley, Arizona.

When I tell people this, they usually chuckle. It occasionally happens when I'm on the phone with someone who needs to get my mailing address. I have, by now, taken to warning them that they will at least smile, if not suppress a giggle or two.

I am uncertain the origin of the name, but there is little doubt there are nights when coyotes begin singing in the desert/golf course area behind our home.

When they sing, it is a sort of discordant harmony sounding a bit like a chorale of sopranos warbling a Gregorian chant in a minor key. As each member runs out of air, they gasp and howl yet once again. Occasionally one of them, apparently not attending to the conductor, ad-libs a "…yip, yip…" solo, only to be quickly overwhelmed, by the larger chorus.

My street, however, is NOT called "Howling Coyote Way" or "Singing Coyote Way," but rather "Laughing Coyote Way."

What is a laughing Coyote? What makes them laugh? Why does something catch their attention in a humorous way? Is it for silly physical comedy, like purposely running into a Saguaro (pronounced 'swa-ro')

Cactus or playing dead - feet straight in the air, tongue hanging out?

When they get tickled, do the corners of their mouths gently curl as their eyes sparkle with subtle anticipation of the impending humor?

Do they tell Coyote jokes to one another? You know,

"Did you hear the one about the jack rabbit, desert rat and wild pig that headed to the creek to get a drink of water?"

"None of them returned…I'm NOT lion!"

Chortle…chortle…yuck…yuck…

There is little doubt there is a lot of material available here in the Sonoran Desert…snakes, big horn sheep, lizards, birds, insects…I mean the wild life is almost immeasurable. "Wild life…" That is in itself a completely different topic. I mean, talk about your party animals…hmm, wild animal nightlife, that would be worth exploring sometime.

But back to the laughing coyotes…

The problem is that these animals are difficult to pin down. It seems this activity happens well after dark when most of us two-legged creatures are tucked away in our dens and temperature controlled caves. Some of us are up at night, but our vision and hearing is so comparatively poor, we long ago decided not to compete with nocturnal creatures hunting for food, entertainment and a good joke now and then.

I suppose, like a lot of other things in my universe, I will have to depend upon someone else's expertise, for it seems the chances of my seeing a Coyote laugh is probably not going to happen.

I have to say, however, I envy that fellow or gal who had the privilege of seeing that event and had the sense to memorialize it "…on the street where I live."

Maybe I could conjure the spirits of George Bernard Shaw (Pygmalion) or Alan Lerner and Fredrick Lowe (musical My Fair Lady) for some catchy lyric/tune…OR simply accept that there are some things in the universe not everyone is privileged to know…

MOMENTS OF REFLECTION

"Realize deeply that the present moment is all you have.
Make the NOW the primary focus of your life."
- Eckhart Tolle, The Power of Now

The temperature had warmed to 32 degrees (0C) on that cold winter's day in New York City. Below 10 degrees (-12C) the night before, we prepared to layer clothing as much as we could – we didn't need as much as we had anticipated.

The journey began with a shuttle to Newark Airport, then the Number 62 bus to Penn Station where we picked up the Port Authority Trans-Hudson (PATH) train for our destination on Manhattan Island. All told, the trip was nearly an hour and a half with the time passing quickly, filled by small talk to cover an undercurrent of somber anticipation.

At the end of the line, we exited the station riding a long escalator from the underground train, embracing the cold winter's air. Out the exit and to our left, we walked around the extremely tall building coming to the place for which we had made this journey:

Ground Zero of the World Trade Center.

"Ground Zero," a term used to describe a point on the earth's surface closest to the detonation of an explosion. On this day, as it turned out, it was both geographic and soulful – the physical site and our hearts...

In Memoriam...
Vesey, Liberty and Church streets framed the memorial fountains – one

for each of the destroyed towers – and subterranean museum sites on three sides with the West Side Highway 'closing the box'…

As we approached the first of the two deeply set fountains, an eerie feeling seeped through my skin…a feeling not so easy to describe, a 'presence' really…a 'knowing'…a disconcerting sensation, communicating the inexpressible magnitude this place had played in our lives and our history.

It wasn't the first time an awareness of 'other presence' had pressed on my spirit. It happened at Dealy Plaza, in the West End District of Dallas where a young American President was assassinated….Auschwitz-Birkenau where the showers of death and work camps of the 'living dead' still resonate in the air…

Here, once again the cloak of discomfort and overwhelming sense of loss oozed through my clothing, both fabric and living, to unbalance the chemistry in my mind.

There is no way to equate these events, but simply a common denominator of holy sobriety covering my soul that I found so unsettling.

We gazed into the pit of the fountains around which names of those lost in the North Tower were engraved, the water at the bottom of this dark cube fell into a smaller and darker cube in its center…lives lost…slipping out of sight…into the abyss…

Hold your mind…don't slip too far into a bottomless pit of thought. I told myself.

The Museum…

We had the time and so purchased tickets for the museum…the intimate memorial…the place in which threads of the end of the lives of real people who had breathed and loved and struggled and failed and succeeded – everyday lives – were woven into an experiential tapestry that will no doubt echo and reverberate and resound in the coming months and years until my breath, as theirs, is finished.

Photo after photo of folks with expressions of disbelief and shock lined the entryway just inside the entrance…a common expression emerging amongst the faces of every race and creed – hands over mouth or on forehead, trying to make sense of the paper and debris floating through the air and to the street below like celebratory confetti, but there was no celebration here.

People had simply been going on about their days with the freedom this country provides, and then…. The event was unthinkable!

The long escalator into the cavernous main museum lay right beside a set of stairs used by some who escaped the unfolding apocalypse…that physically "…escaped the unfolding apocalypse…" – for of little doubt they did not escape leviathan who buried his fearfully long and poisonous talons deeply into their minds that fateful day.

There were so many things in this tomb of memories…fire trucks and ambulances that had been mangled and bent…enormous girders warped and twisted like pieces of taffy…parts of cars and bicycles and shoes worn by people that day.

Along the walls of commemoration were video clips chronicling the unbelievable
series of events…television programs and news casts interrupted,

"In New York City Today, we are getting reports that an
airplane has just crashed into one of the Twin Towers."

"Wait just a minute General, we have actual footage of
the airplane crashing into the North Tower!" Cut to video…

"Alice, this is John," the unknown voice said. "An airplane
has just crashed into the other tower. It's…it's…well, it's
just horrible. We're okay in this tower, I'll call you later, bye."

Of course, John was not okay and the return call to Alice never came.

On the walls were quotes from those who had lost loved ones. The most poignant to me:
"I wished the day would never end, because that day began
with Alan alive, and I wanted to stay in the day he had life."

So much to see…
Animated flight patterns and timelines of the hijackings appeared on walls mesmerizing those watching…histories and flight patterns of the dozen or more flights the terrorists took as they studied the habits of flight attendants and pilots with months of practice runs taken in preparation…all of which was chilling.

In the days following the attack and collapse of the towers, hand made pictures were posted all over the city with variances of these messages - hoping against hope:

"Has anyone seen this man (woman)? If so, please contact___"

"William ____, my father did not come home. If you know anything about him, please call _____"

That day while people *ran from* those buildings, police and firefighters *ran into* them, doing everything in their power to help people escape the ever increasing inferno above. More than four hundred of them died helping others as the buildings collapsed on top of them.

What can be said, really?

This place struck reverence into my heart. It is in moments like this, that one's vocabulary fails to provide anything meaningful to express the magnitude of sobriety and feeling.

There are so many things that are still unfolding in my mind, I am uncertain what to say.

Perhaps I can say this.

Every week, I GET to write whatever I like as I carry on my life, and put it up for public view. Whatever the reader feels about the things I say, I am secure that the 'thought police' will not knock on my door to take me away. This, of course, has not historically nor culturally always been the case.

I am grateful for this, because I understand I only have this moment to think about things I would like to say… this moment to write these thoughts…this moment to appreciate that the unexpected future rushing toward me at light speed, may bring with it...

the unknown…the unthinkable….

HOW ARE YOU LIVING?

> "Our house is a very, very fine house with
> two cats in the yard, life used to be so hard,
> Now everything is easy 'cause of you..."
> - Graham Nash lyricist: <u>Our House</u>

It was a simple abandoned white clapboard two-story house – the photo taken from a low angle on a bleak day emphasizing overgrown weeds and unkempt appearance.

The shot looked to be some 50 to 100 feet away, making this abandoned house appear even more empty...bereft...lonely...cold...unwelcoming.

I never actually saw the house near Nemacolin, Pennsylvania, on route 40 some six miles north, as the crow flies, of the West Virginia border. My friend Ann posted it on social media, and the image was enough to trigger a 'video' from the archives of my mind.

Columbia, Missouri 1974...

I had ridden a few times, but really did not have a lot of experience with horses - Peg did. She was a recent divorcé and I was a student at the beginning of graduate work in Missouri. A mutual friend had set up a horse riding date with her. It turns out the horses were hers and she loved to ride.

That afternoon, we saddled up and rode through unmarked countryside north of Columbia. There were no roads as we trotted through the overgrown fields. I was pleased to be above the brush, certain that had we been walking my ankles would have had scratches looking like an experiment in abstract art.

Somewhere during the ride, in the broad landscape of switchgrass and fescue, stood a two story brownish colored, abandoned and weathered farmhouse standing alone like a long forgotten monument to 'life adventures' past - nothing else in sight.

As we rode closer, you could see through the windows into the three rooms of the downstairs. Standing in the stirrups, I could see the rooms were bone empty.

The overhang of the covered porch was held up by four tired looking posts, their grey color matched by the weathered flooring they covered – grey…worn… uninviting. This place had been sitting for a very long time, and I wondered what stories the walls of that old homestead might have whispered…

Stopping for a few minutes, gaze fixed on that old place, my mind drifted to an imaginary time and imaginary place.

Imagination creates…
I saw a young man and woman beginning their lives together.

Bill and Susan had taken a liking to each other in junior high school, and it continued through high school and university. They married in their 22nd year and looked forward to life together…the sky was blue!

It was the late '60s and Columbia had been the county seat since its incorporation in 1821. It was a university town even then, as in 1839, nine hundred folks pledged nearly $120,00.00 to create the first public university on the western side of the Mississippi River.

By now, the civil war was over and Bill's father built a small mercantile business in which he worked. As was often the case in those days, Bill and Susan lived in the family home in the city. There was room for them all, but they wanted to strike out on their own.

This, of course, was the reason Bill and Susan were looking for a place to call their home.

Somehow they had scraped up enough money to buy a patch of land north of the city. I imagined them sitting around a table somewhere quietly chatting, sparkling with eagerness, about finally having a home of their own.

Then came the day. "I got the loan today Susan!" he said, his heart racing with excitement.

"I'm taking a chance here," Mr. Jenkins the banker had said. "But you are a hard worker, Bill and your family have been solid citizens here in Columbia."

Bill negotiated with Samuel Johnson, the landowner, and the deal was done!

Later they built this two-story house…insulated the walls and painted it a bright white! It wasn't a palace, but it was theirs, and on weekends they would walk the land talking about their future.

The house was pretty big for just the two of them, but they had plans and in the third and fourth years in the life of that house…no that would be wrong…their home, she delivered children, Bill junior, followed the next year by Elizabeth – Betsy to her friends, but that would come later.

In the 10th year of their marriage the front porch came and Susan painted the flooring a rustic brown, making those four posts multicolored with white, green and light redish bands. Against the background of the house, they could be seen from quite a distance by folk who came to visit. Susan had a quiet flare.

She loved that porch and on quiet afternoons, when Bill was at work and the children in school, she would sit in the rocker Bill surprised her with on her 34th birthday, and let her mind drift to her children, husband and gratitude for this place 'they' built, loved and lived in.

Bill died in his 67th year of an unexpected heart attack. The children, now grown and living in Columbia, tried unsuccessfully to get Susan to move to town with them.

She had steadfastly resisted…this was her home…this is what she knew…this is where everything meaningful in her life had happened.

"No, dears," she said, "I belong here…I will be fine."

She wasn't fine, of course. Even though she was in her home where it all had happened, it was by now empty and she was alone. In truth, she felt empty too.

They found her sitting in her rocking chair on the front porch, grey hair fluttering in the breeze, her head bowed, lifeless eyes closed as if she were in prayer – she was, you know.

It was a warm Sunday morning in June, a year to the day that Bill had died…they had come to take her to church. No one would know how long that year had been for her, but now they were together again…

The homestead? Well, the kids had families of their own, yet that sturdy old house wasn't going anywhere and though it could have been given better attention, it stood its ground to the autumn day Peg and I rode by.

Horses, houses and fields…
"That place must be over a 100 years old," Peg said breaking my daydream and bringing me back to the present starkness of this open and scrub filled landscape upon which the old house had been built, full of love and sorrow – the kind that comes to all of us…the kind that gives our existence texture and richness.

It was time to go, so we headed back to her place, wiped the horses down, put them in the barn. I thanked Peg for the day and headed home.

Later that night as I sat in my little efficiency apartment, I thought about Bill and Susan. They were, nothing more than figments of my imagination, but they had 'come' to my mind…drifted through as though we were friends with a history.

When I saw that house sitting on the prairie, I experienced my own desire for stability…my own yearning for a place I could call home…my own need for solid ground under my feet…something reliable – something constant.

Over the years, I have come to appreciate 'places' DO NOT…CAN NOT…provide a sense of comfort. It is never about the place, – it wasn't for my Bill and Susan – rather it was the love…the care…the human connections between…

That picture posted by my friend, reminded me how easy it is to let our houses (minds) sit quietly while the paint fades and the life that once was slowly drifts away. It takes work, commitment and a little fresh paint now and then to make our house a home and inviting…

"Coffee on the porch anyone? I have an extra rocker…"

UNEXPECTED LESSONS

> "And Moses was content to dwell with the man:
> and he gave Moses Zipporah his daughter."
> - Exodus 2:21, Bible

He was big and he was smart.

When he knocked her to the ground, he just walked away 10 feet or so and waited. She got up a little unsteady on her feet; he walked over and knocked her down again.

The setting...

Nearly 30 years of my life centered around a small acre of land on highway 24 West in the rural community of Moberly, Missouri. I came to a small Bible teaching community in 1975, in the second year of my doctoral program at the University of Missouri. The school program would take two or three years, and I had found a place where I could do a little scripture studying at the same time. After the war and a few years of school, I was restless and it seemed like a good fit. While I didn't know it at the time, those two or three years would turn into three decades!

In the early years, while in school, I lived in a trailer on the church property with a couple of other fellows. I am not sure I have either the time, or the hard drive space, to recount the many adventures and stories that occurred in those thirty years, but on this Christmas day I am reminded of Moses and Zipporah...not Moses and Zipporah of the Old Testament scriptures, but Moses and Zipporah the dogs!

Oh the weather out side is frightful...

It was winter in Missouri...a winter that had brought a lot of snow. Not that powdery kind that comes from freezing temperatures high in the atmosphere...the kind that dusts the ski slopes of the Colorado Rockies. Rather the wet heavy kind that happens when temperatures in the clouds are at or just above freezing.

This kind of snow creates a '...deafening silence...' found in soundproof rooms – you know the kind. It falls fast and in big flakes...the kind that comes on the heels of a few mild winter days...the kind that snarls traffic in cities and towns...the kind that packs down and makes the county and state roads deadly...the kind that overcomes the best battle plans of the salt and gravel trucks...the kind that replaces the snow as fast as a plow can clear it, AND the kind that lends itself to wonderful snowmen, angels in the snow, and enthusiastic snowball fights. Yes sir, the kind that brings out the child in all but the grumpiest of folk who always see the glass half empty!

My friend Moses...

It was winter and a time of year that Moses seemed to love. While he officially belonged to David, he was for all practical purposes the 'church dog.' He was a large German shepherd weighing in somewhere north of 85 pounds (38k). He looked big under normal circumstances, but in moments of alarm, when his body hair stood on end – he looked enormous and it was breath taking!

The church property sat right on the highway. It was the kind of road farmers and others used to get to town and back...the kind of road that claimed the lives of countless cats and dogs finding themselves unwisely crossing in search of a mouse or other small animal living in the surrounding woods. For some reason Moses, had learned to look both ways...he understood death lurked on that ribbon of asphalt running beside the trailer where he lived, and he had a healthy respect for it.

In those early years, Moses was a fixture. While his real home was a pen beside the trailer, he was allowed inside, and there were many nights he stayed with me in that trailer.

Stray animals were not unusual...

Over the years a lot of stray dogs and cats made their way on to the church property – many stayed until the highway or greener pastures either ended their lives or caused them to move on. Moses pretty much put up with them. Putting up meant...if they didn't bother him, he wouldn't bother them. He had seen a lot in his years and seemed to understand détente was the best policy.

During the fall of this year, Zipporah arrived at church. In the scriptures, Zipporah was a Midianitish woman that Moses married. In Moberly, Missouri, she was simply a dog!

By the time she arrived, Moses was a little old to consider her, in the politest of terms, mating material. She was skittish and very timid. In spite of this, Moses tried to engage her. Yet, almost every time he came near, she would assume a submissive posture and cower.

Old dogs teaching new tricks…

The trailer in which I lived was on the Eastern edge of, and parallel to, the parking lot. This morning, because of the snow, there were no cars other than those parked the night before. I had wakened and was in the process of trying to determine whether I should head over to the church for coffee. I glanced out the window to see how much snow had fallen and saw Moses and Zipporah standing in the center of the car park.

Moses walked over to her, and as she started to assume the position, he knocked her down. He then walked away and stood still. When she got up a little unsteadily to her feet; he walked over and knocked her down again. This happened three or four times.

For some reason, Zipporah seemed to want to make peace. With head down, she cautiously made her way to Moses and sniffed at him. As her nose touched his side, he collapsed to the ground. This startled her and she jumped back. Moses got up and trotted another 10 feet away or so and stood still…Zipporah made her way uneasily toward him again. As before, when she sniffed at him and as her nose touched his coat, he fell to the ground.

This cycle repeated itself several times until Zipporah seemed to 'get it.' She realized this was a game, and within the 15 minutes or so as I watched this amazing event, she was running at Moses, <u>trying to knock him down</u>! The next few minutes, the dogs played in the snow – the youngster and the old man – as though they were both pups. Moses quit first…she flat wore him out!

I don't know how animals think, or how they process information, but it is my sense Moses wished he had never taught that dog to play. For in the few remaining months/years of his life, Zipporah was unrelenting in her attention for him. She would tug at him trying to get him to play with her. From her perspective, I suppose it was simply unbridled affection…

Moses? Had he known Greek mythology, he might have felt he had opened Pandora's box, producing a creature that gave him no peace. From time to time, he would have an expression in his eyes that seemed to say, "What have I created!" And yet, I am certain, given the opportunity, he would have done it all again. For me, watching that old dog teaching a life lesson to Zipporah was one of the more unexpected pleasures of my life.

The Christmas season, in spite of all the stresses that come along with it, is a time to be grateful for the health that we have and the life we have been given…a time to be gentle with one another and remember those we love…a time to appreciate the circumstances in our lives that have touched us in meaningful ways…big and small.

I am grateful for my family, and the people from all over this world God has brought into and enriched my life…there is little doubt, however, in the tapestry of my experiences and corner of my heart, where the brush strokes are subtle and barely noticeable to the casual observer…Moses gently resides.

LOVE, ROLLER COASTERS AND LITTLE GIRLS

> "No one is smart enough to figure out
> anything worthwhile from scratch."
> - Pinker, S. The Better Angels of our Nature

Susie Shamkunas (Sham-Koo-nis)…now there is a name, and there was a girl. Little doubt, I was smitten!

Memory is that illusive narrator of history with a kind of plasticity. You know, elastic things return to their original shape (rubber bands, for example), plastic changes DO NOT return to their original shape (pie crust from a ball of dough). Once changed, they appear to have always been that way. Yeah, memory may or may not have anything to do with the truth.

Truth – what the heck is the truth?

But then there was Susie Shamkunas, at the age of six, the love of my life. In my less mature years (prior to six), I thought girls were…hmmm…in the nicely honed vocabulary of my youth - YUCKIE! In fact, I even resented them in the free floating anxiety best expressed by having been isolated to my own bedroom, while my sisters got to share. I didn't understand and thought it to be completely unfair!

Girls, as far as I could tell, were a real nuisance.

The page turned…
But then something changed, something brand new, something I had even less understanding about – I 'saw' Susie. It wasn't that I had not seen her before, after all, we were in Sunday school together.

I don't even know when this actually happened, but one day I looked at her and all kinds of things began to happen: unsettled tummy, short breath, heart beat faster, no words to speak, damp hands and furtive glances to see if there were some place to hide!

Yep, I think I was in love! She had blond curly hair, wore frilly dresses, had brown eyes, and I don't know…it was like I had been lightening struck.

One day, when my mother was looking after her at our house – right at the beginning of the Mickey Mouse Club on TV – I kissed her! Okay, I had been emboldened by Annette Funicello, whose face had just popped up on the screen announcing herself: "Annette!"

I had practiced kissing Annette on a couple of occasions when she announced herself, so I did have experience.

I mumbled something like, "I love you and now you are my girlfriend."

She smiled and giggled like we had just shared a secret, and I can't remember one other thing about the girl from that day forward! The event with Susie is memorable to me, simply because…well, simply because of the feelings and the terror of the first kiss!!

I loved my mother and dad, but would characterize that as a feeling of consistency and safety. I know I learned to love my sisters, I suppose because they were daily constants in the routine of my life, but I can say this with certain authority – I NEVER felt anything with my family like I felt with that cutie pie who first stole my heart – Susie Shamkunas!

Yeah, but what does it mean?

Love! That set of feelings that have yet to be defined despite the untold volumes of poetry, stories, music and film on the subject – all of which reflect the most common and primal sensations every single one of us has had. Importantly, when read, heard or seen, some ageless resonance is touched within us and we know with a surety we have at least basked in the echoed shadow of the 'vérité obscure' (obscure truth).

So what is this thing called love. One is tempted to express, "I don't exactly know what it is, but I know it when I see [feel] it!"

Okay, to be fair, there are dictionary definitions categorizing the attraction we, as humans have for one another: *affection, friendship, romance, eros and unconditional love.* I suppose I can identify with these words in terms of the way we interact with one another, and I further suppose, for this discussion, I'm talking about eros…I guess.

Giving it a whirl…

I have given this a fair amount of thought in trying to understand the context of my life experience. I mean, when does the 'I like you' slip over the cliff to 'I love you'?

"Cliff" is a good metaphor, best reflected in the expression "…falling in love…" Yeah, that's the feeling isn't it – falling! Like the first drop on one of those huge rollercoasters.

If you are a kindred spirit that likes coasters, close your eyes and imagine the excitement of heading up the first hill, the tearful anticipation of the approaching uncontrolled feelings, the exhilaration as the car passes the crest and the total cognitive 'short circuitry' of the drop!

No thought…no deliberation…no sense of anything but the astonishing stomach turning of the drop! Yeah, that's what I think love is…or at least how it seems to start.

The thing is, everything we know comes into our minds single file, and every way we communicate with others, comes out of us single file…but man, when all that stuff is 'in the mixer,' Katy bar the door! When the accumulated paraphernalia floating around in our brains is sparked by feelings of love – all bets are off! Call it Kismet, pheromones, serendipity, fate, the weather, the stars…call it whatever you want, but when it is lit 'things' happen!

Empires built, novels written, songs sung, flights to the moon and the stars, an explosions of creativity – a 'no holds barred' sensation overcomes us and we feel there is NOTHING we cannot do!

The 'language of love,' usually in the context of the delicate – sometimes not so delicate – dance that leads to a carnally conclusive act, is often discussed as though sexual gratification were the driving force toward the end game whispered by our genetic code for the survival of the species. Yeah, maybe…

All I know is that when it gets going – Mazel Tov!! (Congratulations and Good luck!!)

As the management of those initial feelings, Plato calls the 'charioteer' of our nature, emerge...the wilder horse is reined in by the driver (human soul), and once happening, our widely swinging feelings calm (the more noble horse taking control) and our lives proceed forward.

There is more...
The thing is, we are not machines. The passion of love that we feel in the beginning doesn't (or shouldn't) go away and can emerge at any time in our lives. In maturity, it may become more guarded and 'other focused' through the accomplishment of tasks/goals/challenges life brings us, but the appetite of the wild horse lying just under the surface continues to inform the things we do and decisions we make.

This may be a revelation to those of you who are young, but while planetary 'time in service' may diminish many things, it does NOT lessen feelings of passion.

Take away...
So what is my take away from this? I have come to believe the passion of love is like beautiful music the lyrics for which we have not yet, as a species, come to truly understand...or at least in a succinct, clear, articulated way.

I think love is a primal communication that God, the universal creative intelligence, has placed in us as a homing mechanism to draw us toward one another yes, but more importantly, closer toward Him.

Love has no time...no distance...no culture...no circumstance...no geography defining its existence. It may begin with proximity, but from the 'lighting of the fuse,' it has a life of its own.

You don't believe this? Take a moment to think about someone you love(ed) with whom you no longer have contact, or who may have passed on from this life...take a moment and think of them...what do you feel?

Yeah, I thought so.

I can tell you this...when Susie Shamkunas came to mind, it wasn't some distant thought of 'Paradise Lost,' it was with all the richness, sincerity and feelings a little boy of six could muster...

OUR LIFE IS A VAPOR

> "See her how she flies golden sails across the sky
> Close enough to touch but careful if you try
> Though she looks as warm as gold
> The moon's a harsh mistress
> The moon can be so cold."
> - Jimmy Web: Song writer
> The moon's a harsh mistress

This time she had a gun, dramatically changing the dynamics. You see, when you have a gun, AND the authorities get involved…all of it – and I mean all of it – takes on a life of its own.

There were a couple of police officers at the rear of her home when we left in the early morning to exercise. By the time we returned, there were nearly 100, a SWAT team in full battle array carrying AR-15s, and the Bomb Squad…all focused on our friend hoping, in the end, she could be talked down.

You see, when you have a gun, AND the authorities get involved…all of it takes on a life of its own…

Another day…
The morning started like most. Turn on the coffee, feed the cats, get a cup of coffee, sit and read for a while.

Actually, before the read, sometimes I check the overnight news headlines and emails to see what the coming day might be bringing.

To: my email in box - 6:04AM

"Ted, if I do not answer the door by late this afternoon, please feed the cats."

To: Gail 6:05AM

"I was just thinking of you…will do…"

Gail and I have known each other for a couple of years, but friends since arriving in our little Oro Valley neighborhood the last year. She is a smart, thoughtful, engaging and richly deep person in her expression of thought – a retired administrator by trade, living what could be called an idyllic and genteel retirement. A relative youngster in her mid sixties, her working life successes had allowed her to walk away early and with some comfort.

She is a Buddhist and has found a 'place' in the universe that is gratifying when we 'close the outside doors' and jump into one another's minds to see what the 'collective interaction' might discover. Winding through the chasms and 'blue highways' of her knowledgeable wealth has always been a delight. I have not engaged her once, and not felt the benefit of her gifts and wisdom. Our time together is resonant and well spent.

She is a small woman…slight of stature, with greyish hair that hangs a little more than halfway to her shoulders. When engaged, her bright eyes sparkle with focus and interest.

Gail is a private person, who lets you 'in' on her terms and does so without apology. Sometimes people, careful about access to their lives, come across abrupt and unfriendly. Not so Gail. She just has that kind of aura that says, "I have worked hard to create a world in which I feel safe and comfortable. This is the way I most easily manage the "…doors of perception…" in my life. It doesn't mean I don't like or want to be around you, I just like to take life in small bites…"

I love that about her!

The three of us – Molly, Gail and I – have a relaxed relationship; one of easy acceptance. She is a cat lover, and as it turned out an avid sports enthusiast. When the sport conversations begin between the girls, I slip into a 'different room,' for in that arena, by comparison, I am a rank amateur.

Gail has had Meniere's disease for the last 6 years or so. It is an ailment of the inner ear that causes extreme dizziness, often accompanied with hearing loss, ringing in the ears and sometimes pressure. In her case, the pressure manifests as pain…strong and unrelenting pain.

Finally, last month, it was too much and she took an overdose of potent medication with the intent of ending her pain AND her life…or so it seemed, but uncharacteristically she left her garage door open and front door unlocked, sending a small alarm through this neighbor friendly community. We got to her in time and she survived.

Out of the hospital for a little better than a week, she was doing pretty well. We had, as usual, a long open ended chat a couple of days ago and a short one yesterday. No hint – no warning.

My inbox: "Ted, if I do not answer the door by late this afternoon, please feed the cats."

This morning after her email, she made a call to the local crisis hotline; that triggered the police interdiction protocol, and probably saved her life. It took several hours before she 'gave it up' and was taken to the hospital for a minimum 96-hour hold. You see, it is not against the law to take your own life…I mean, what IS the punishment??

This is not the first friend who contacted me when it looked like it was the end of the road for them. It has happened a time or two…one survived and has carried on, as far as I can tell, a productive and healthy life…one did not.

A time for thought…
I have spent a good part of the day thinking about this against the tapestry of the final three years or so of my mother's life – a brilliant, thoughtful, compassionate and caring person – caught in the ever-darkening prison of Alzheimer's disease.

I also watched as my younger sister, the brightest and best of our family, slowly strangled…each breath more labored…in the throes of early onset Alzheimer's until she died in the most undignified way, while we stood in sorrowful impotence, quietly to the end.

The miracles of modern medicine? It is hard for me to imagine a more cruel and merciless way for these women to have ended their journey.

I have heard the arguments for the sanctity of human life…for letting the 'will of God' take its course…hell, I have made them myself…yet over the years, these words have rung more and more hollow.

It seemed so easy to advise and pontificate about the value of 'climbing the rope' to the very end. It seemed so easy until I was on that rope...so easy until I was uncertain what to do...until I watched in horror as two women, one of whom brought me to life and the other who knew me better than any living creature...watching like a guard over the prison of the condemned, awaiting their execution.

But you see, there was NO EXECUTION! There was only the agonizing and unrelenting, breath and life taking experience of waiting...waiting...waiting until every good and gracious characteristic was stolen with the painfully slow 'skin stripping' of death's gravitational pull...pulled to and from their very last breaths!

The neighborhood...

"This time she had a gun, dramatically changing the dynamics. You see, when you have a gun, AND the authorities get involved...all of it – and I mean all of it – takes on a life of its own...."

Gail? I cannot say into what dark place she found herself hopelessly huddled as she twice contemplated the end of her journey. I can't even say it was a dark place...I am no jury...I am no judge.

I can and will say this.

When she returns home, I (we) will continue to love and support her as long as she is with us. If it is a long time, I will no doubt be the beneficiary of this bright and articulate woman's mind.

If it is not a long time, I will take consolation in the moments we shared and as God IS MY WITNESS, I will not blame her for decisions she makes or thoughts to which I am not privy nor understand, nor will I feel guilty that my voice and the voices of others, were not enough to make a difference.

After all...she is a private woman and she is my friend.

RANDOM ACTS

"If you love somebody, you had
better hurry up and tell them."
– Author Unknown

He was riding his bicycle on the service road just off Interstate 5 when a car left the freeway, came down an embankment and hit him straight on taking his life!

What are the odds??

I'm not sure what the fellow was thinking when he got up that morning and headed out for a ride. I am not sure what the woman driver was thinking as she headed north on the interstate. I am certain, neither one of them expected to find themselves in proximity under any circumstances!

Maybe the guy was thinking about work, or breakfast, or his family or the music he was listening to…the woman hurrying to work or the store or coming home from dropping off her kids…whatever. Of all the things these two people could have conceived, in their wildest imaginations…the darkest places in the depths of their brains…this…this would NEVER have emerged into their consciousness, and yet here it was…their lives would never be the same, and I mourned for them.

Why them? Why then? Why not someone else? Why not somewhere else? Why not one minute sooner or one minute later? The unpredictability and random acts of life exceed storylines even the most creative writers could dig out of the recesses of their minds.

This could have been anyone…it could have not happened at all.

A memory…

It was Vietnam…the early fall of 1969 and by now after nearly a year of my tour had passed. I had found ways to compensate for being in this strange land. A prime example was learning to sleep. I had self-talked that I was safe, that if something happened it would be to someone else. Fantasy? Sure, but one does whatever it takes to normalize in the most abnormal of situations.

I was an air traffic controller in the military and had adapted to the unnatural sounds of airplanes landing on a runway not more than 200 yards (183m) from my 'hooch' – the name for the plywood barracks in which we were housed. Sleeping was also challenged during the rainy season. There is little louder than the mind numbing decibels of monsoon rain hitting a metal roof. One had to practically yell to hold a conversation with the person next to them. Even then I found a way to touch that gracious 'gift of the gods' and fall asleep.

It is said there are two categories of people in this world…those that move dirt, and those that supervise the dirt movers. In Vietnam, we moved a lot of dirt.

It had been a late night, and I had spent the evening at the non-commissioned officer's (NCO) club with my best friend Bob – I slept hard.

They said the hooch took a direct hit…the navy commander probably hadn't heard a thing and had been killed outright. They said it was his last day 'in country.' He was preparing to head home…no mission to fly, but a flight to catch departing this airfield for the last, "Thank God Almighty" time.

I wondered about that man and wrote some of these thoughts then…

What had he been thinking as he counted down the days. I wondered how many missions he had flown and how many times his life had been at risk…I wondered how often he had thanked God for a safe return to base and the cold beer in his hand to celebrate another day burned from the calendar.

There were rituals…

We did this you know…we counted days…we celebrated when there were fewer left than there had been to stay – at first the fear of too many days ahead, with too many chances…chances for something bad to happen; then too few days with heightened sense of excitement that home grew closer, but fear that it would be snatched away at the last minute. Even getting on that plane with 200 plus other dirty smelly GIs at the end of the tour, there was the risk of being shot down as the aircraft took off. No sir, no sigh of relief until the airspace of the Republic of South Vietnam was somewhere in the distance behind us.

Continuing the thought…

In the early morning hours, the navy commander's life was snatched away at the last minute…he would not be catching that flight home…at least not the one he had been anticipating. The string of life severed from 'his instrument' in the universe, no longer resonating in measured harmony with anything…with anyone.

I wondered what he might have been thinking as he got up that morning. Maybe he had been dreaming of his family and how great it would be to breathe the fresh and familiar air of his home. Maybe he was sitting on the edge of his bunk putting on his boots, in uniform for the last time…looking forward.

I didn't hear the rockets. I had learned to sleep…sleep in this 'Alice Through the Looking Glass' country, through most anything. Me? I was dreaming about my family at home and how great it would be to breathe the fresh and familiar air of my hometown. On that morning I sat on the edge of my bunk, put on my jungle boots, in uniform for yet another day and headed for breakfast.

When I heard the news, I was struck by the complete and utter unpredictability of life…He was gone, his family's lives would never be the same, and I mourned him.

The car did not come off the freeway that year and hit my bicycle…it hit that navy commander's.

I wondered, why his hooch, not mine? Why him, not me? Why not later or sooner?

Each of us has stories of the randomness of life…the unexpected moments that change everything. Not all are lethal…many act to change life in the most remarkable of ways…These kinds of things, however, remind me to appreciate and try and be as much in the 'moment' as possible…because one never knows…

HERE BE DRAGONS

"The two most important days in your life are the
day you are born and the day you find out why."
- Mark Twain

Dateline: Singapore - October 12, 2014, 9:45PM

It was late...it has been a long day...we were tired.

We hesitated, because of the lateness of the hour, but decided to go for dinner at Boat Quay (pronounced 'key') on the Southwestern edges of the Singapore River.

This area is lined with outdoor restaurants, serving pretty much any style food one might desire, and since this was Asia, all of it was tasty. We would need only to pick the style of food and settle in at a table along the riverbank to finish the day, relax and enjoy the sights, sounds and smells of this wonderfully exotic place.

We had just gotten out of a taxi on Lor Telok Street, when we heard a roar that sounded like an athletic event. It got a little quiet and then started up again.

"Let's go see what's going on, " Andry said.

So, we headed away from the Quay to North Canal, turned right and walked the 400 feet or so to New Bridge Road, where looking both right and left, there were people as far as the eye could see. One half of the road was blocked off with barriers, behind which there seemed to be hundreds, maybe thousands of men. As we watched, the men moved from our right to our left stopped…moved and stopped. It was a curious sight.

Ask and ye shall receive…
"Pardon me sir," I said to the man in the yellow reflective vest, looking like a parade Marshall.

"What is going on here?"

Just then, a similarly dressed man opened the gate to a very large rectangular shaped corral holding more than 100, 'ground sitting' men in traditional loincloths…some wearing tee shirts – others shirtless.

They instantly jumped to their feet and with a shouting frenzy exploded out of the containment area, running full tilt to the next containment area where they sat down on the ground again. This sequence repeated itself again and again like pulsing of blood through the circulatory system…each beat moving the life giving liquid further and further down the arterial tree.

"This is the Thimithi festival done every year here in Singapore," the man said.

Timing is everything…
Thimithi is the annual Fire Walking festival attracting hundreds of thousands of Hindu devotees in a number of countries. Fire walking has been a tradition with the Hindu faithful for over 1,000 years. It is done in remembrance of a woman named Druapadi, whose honor was saved by Krishna, when she was about to be shamed by a cousin in the famous Sanskrit philosophic Epic and story of the Kurukshetra wars titled: Mahabharata.

In Singapore, it happens in October…this year the 12th, our late evening dinner night!

The processions begin around 10PM at Sri Srinivasa Perumal Temple on Serangoon Road and end at Sri Mariamman Temple on South Bridge Road, where the hot coal beds await the focused minds and feet of the faithful!

If one were to walk the route, it would take a little under an hour, but with nearly 10,000 Hindu faithful men preparing to 'walk the fire' at the Sri Mariamman Temple, the event takes hours to complete, with the primary travel routes closed to traffic from mid afternoon through 7AM the following morning.

Not for the faint of heart...

These worshippers were in a heightened state of excitement, and while they obediently sat waiting for the gates to open to make their way toward their final destination where they would 'walk the fire,' it seemed clear they were in a 'different world.' It is difficult to explain how fearfully impressive this event was...literally controlled mayhem!

To the outsider, and that would be me, there was the sense that if a crowd of 10,000 people began to move and take on a life of its own, whoever or whatever was in the path would simply be overwhelmed and crushed. I have watched large crowd demonstrations on television, but this...being there...feeling the throb...sensing both safety and danger of the unknown...was a window into the exotic and an experience of a lifetime.

We followed on the sidewalk, beside this pulsating mass of men, toward the Sri Mariamman Temple, wanting to see them walk the hot coals. We were, however, not the only ones interested. As we got closer to the Temple the sidewalk became more and more congested, so that by the time we got near the Temple doors we were literally stuck in a crushing mass of people, packed so close together it was almost impossible to move.

Andry and I both sensed we should probably not stay there, so pushing and shoving a little; we made our away back against the press of people trying to get into the event, and within minutes we were gratefully free of the crushing mass of humanity.

Dinner on the Quay...

We made our way back the eight blocks or so along South Bridge Road until we got to South Canal and to a restaurant along at Boat Quay, where we shared a large rectangular pan of spicy soup, Chinese noodles and a wonderfully cooked whole fish.

As we sat along the bank of the river and quietly chatted, looking across the brightly lighted harbor, we were energized by the sense of wonder and a little danger from the adventure.

The tiredness we felt earlier in the evening had evaporated from an unexpected event we had just witnessed, and we were both grateful we had not been too tired to eat. The evening's meal and unexpected undertaking, satisfied our stomach and our minds....

PEBBLES DROP – RIPPLES NEVER END

> Old men start 'em and
> young men fight 'em"
> - Many renditions

"Hi," I said. "I heard you guys were part of the Vietnam Veterans Association."

I had just approached a group of men sitting at the breakfast table at the Hilton El Conquistador Resort in Tucson, Arizona, in the summer of 2002.

It was the last day of a spine conference, and I was eating breakfast with some folk from the organization for whom I had spoken. Someone at my table mentioned the fellows across the room were part of a Vietnam veterans group that would be starting their conference on the following day.

Never the wallflower, I thought I would say hi.

"My name is Ted, and although I haven't done much with the veterans groups, I thought I would come over and say hello."

"I don't know where you all served, but I was a 'Spec 5' in the First Aviation Brigade in Vung Tau…1969-'70."

For a few moments they just looked at me and said nothing…

Memory trigger…
This memory began at the bank earlier in the week, when Molly and I

were changing some accounts around. I don't do much with the finances in my family...I have always believed one should let the person with the appropriate skill set manage the things they know best. Molly? Well, she trained as an engineer and then did an accounting degree with a CPA certification...

I thought, in the early days, for the briefest of milliseconds, I could help with the finances of the household – you know collaborate as a team, but it was clear the approach of rounding up to the nearest dollar in my checkbook as I had done when I was single would not play as a 'team sport' – Molly handles ALL things financial!

Adam D. is our current banker, and this week, because I needed to be there in person to execute some documents, we met for the first time. It turns out he was a delightful young man...chatty...friendly...AND it was clear he and Molly had a well-oiled yearlong relationship.

It turns out he was a veteran of six years and had taken three tours to Afghanistan/Iraq during his time in the military. Sometimes getting banking things done takes a little time with 'waiting spaces,' between signatures, so we had a few moments to get to know one another.

Adam had been a plumber in the military, a bartender and a banker in civilian life. He was in his early thirties and in spite of his beard he had a youthful appearance and an open nature that was compelling. His eyes, however, told a different story...they were windows to his soul that had recorded things in the hard disks of his mind that took some years of counseling to talk through... post traumatic stress? Yes sir! When he spoke about this, 'the rooms of my mind' got silent as the closed vault doors of the bank in which we were seated. For a few moments the rooms of our minds found 'a place' and there was no one in his small office, but he and I.

There is a brother/sisterhood in the men and women who have served this country in military conflict...a bridge over which those who have not had that experience, are unable to cross. A 'knowing'...a kind of unseen set of tentacles reaching from the unconsciousness of one to the other, and regardless of one's life experience or circumstance of the moment, touching something deep...something unspoken.

I liked this young man right away, and I think he liked me.

The story...
In the course of the conversation I said, "You know I had this

experience with a group of guys here in Tucson a little over a decade ago, long before we moved here."

I began…

"Hi," I said. "I heard you guys were part of the Vietnam Veterans Association…"

For a few moments they just looked at me and said nothing…

It was a little strange.

Then, without a word, one of the fellows from across the table got up, walked around to me, put out his hand and looked me straight in the eye.

"Welcome home," he said as only one who knew could. "I'm John S." He then gave me his rank, where and when he served in Vietnam.

As he was finishing, a second man silently got up and walked around the table extending his hand. "Welcome home," he gently said, giving his name and the particulars of his service in that far off land.

There were six men at that table, and each of them, 'one by one,' stood from their seats, came to me and repeated the words that none of us had heard when we returned from that distant place where none of us wanted to be – to the "…land of the free and the home of the brave." Truth be told, I had never heard them from anyone other than my parents when they held their only son, safely home, in their arms – until that day…it had been 32 years and change.

Everything gets recorded…
I am certain these men had made a habit of touching that vacant and hungry spot they knew to be in the hearts of other veterans…the spot covered over by time and circumstance until its presence no longer anywhere in sight…the spot buried in the land of Oz – into the unresolved clutter of "…it is what it is…"

Yeah, I'm pretty certain this was not the first time they had done this for a comrade in arms…and yet…and yet, when those words were spoken, those 'knowing eyes' engaged mine, and hands encircled mine…it was these men who touched that spot – that spot that had for so many years longed to be acknowledged…it was these knowing men who provided a kind of closure for which I cannot find words.

To be frank, there was not a dry eye in the seven – six of them and me – from that heartfelt connection.

Back to the bank...
I have thought of this story from time to time over the years, and told it a time or two, BUT the morning at the Bank with Adam was the first time I had shared it with another Veteran...a young man with whom I shared a common bond. To be frank, neither of us had dry eyes.

"Thanks for your service," is a common phrase for our veterans in this day and time, and while I am sure it is a sincere gesture on the part of those that say it...there is a certain intimacy...a rich and deeply felt sense of fraternity and appreciation for the words spoken by those Veterans on that morning, in that restaurant, at that hotel in Tucson in 2002.

I looked across the desk at this young man...

"Welcome home Adam..."

LET THERE BE PEACE

"In memory, everything seems to happen to music."
- Tennessee Williams: The Glass Menagerie

It began with 11 simple words posted on Carol's Facebook page.

"Let there be peace on earth and let it begin with me…"

In less than a millisecond I disappeared into the mists of memory finding two companions significant to my life: My older sister Anne and my mother.

For the next 10 or 15 minutes, I entered the 'cavern of cognitive dissociation' from the real world, and was transported to any number of settings where the beginning lines to this family favorite brought images and sounds, with clarity, to my heart and mind.

In those moments lost to reality, these two wonderful women sang this hymn for me under very different circumstances. Anne was gifted from a child with a notable soprano voice. My father liked to show her off when people visited, and I cannot count the number of times he, to my mind, aggressively encourage her to sing for our guests.

She may have enjoyed this – I never really asked – but it seemed to me, she often sang under duress. I do know this, however, she loved music and loved to sing and cultivated her gift through a graduate degree in voice, making a career of pleasing people privileged to hear her and cultivating the gifts of voice students with whom she has spent her adult life teaching.

My mother, on the other hand, had a lovely 'choir' voice. It was in the alto register and quietly expressive. As a child and young adult, she had memorized many hymns, the words of which brought her strength and sustenance. She sang and taught them to me…it was her way.

When I read the single line post, my mother's voice took over my mind with an almost startling immediacy and I heard her with quiet sincerity sing those words to me once again. It was as though I had slipped into a tub of warm water and felt the soothing gentleness of her character envelop me as she so often had done in her life.

Anne then appeared with a power and inspiration of voice that one could not hear without being touched. This song and 'You'll Never Walk Alone' (also a favorite of Mum) came to mind with the rush of a summer wind blowing through the leaves of the Canadian hardwood trees of my youth. I suppose because it seemed so natural to hear her sing, I seldom expressed to her the depths with which her voice touched me.

It gets better…
I was so taken by Carol's first line, that I posted the next …"Let there be peace on earth – the peace that was meant to be."

Over the next day, other friends of hers placed line after line – one person at a time until the first verse was complete. I confess, I checked several times during the day, hoping it would get done.

While the specific circumstance was unexpected and greatly enjoyed, the experience of an unpredicted stimulus bringing to life things passed, is not new to me, and I am certain, you either. It is part of the magic of life!

The bigger picture…
I never cease to be fascinated that everything entering through the vacuum cleaners of sight, sound, touch, smell and taste, somehow sticks to fluid bathed, micro electric neurons and remains surprisingly alive and well somewhere in what appear to be inaccessible regions of our minds…until…until some unforeseen stimulus brings them to the surface like bobbing balloons held under water and quickly released.

The thing is, we don't ask for these memories to emerge, from behind the boulders and sand dunes of our minds. Yet there they reside, in what seems to be a state of suspended animation eagerly waiting for an opportunity to slip across the Technicolor, silver screens of our minds.

I had not expected to spend a little time with the women of my family yesterday. In fact, I can't think of anything that was further from my mind, or maybe better said, buried more deeply in my mind.

More to the point, I had certainly not expected to see the first line of that wonderful old hymn on Carol's Facebook page either. Yet post it she did and with little doubt, the quality of my day was immeasurably better…

NO ONE THINKS

"Jesus Christ, this kid is dying!"

Not the words a person is interested in hearing, particularly if they happen to be 'the kid.'

It was two AM in Vung Tau, the Republic of Vietnam – 1969. I was working the night shift alone as a radar air traffic controller and napping in our small portable radar unit. The radios were on, in case an aircraft called in.

Unbeknownst to me a small centipede had crawled under my tee shirt. Unfortunately, it was poisonous and bit the inside of my arm while I slept. I didn't realize it was there, but the bite woke me up. My left arm was numb as often happens when you lie on your side, so I shook it out. The numbness did not go away and I began to feel sick.

A call into base operations sent a couple of my co-workers to pick me up and take me to the medical facility – a large sectioned off tent. By thr time I arrived, the little creature still under my shirt had bitten me twice more. Over the next twenty minutes or so, lying on an observation cot, my breathing became a little shallower and pupils began to constrict. The medics decided to wake the doctor on call, who felt I should be given an injection of epinephrine (adrenaline) used for situations of developing shock.

The problem? He gave me more than he should have. Within a breath, I was in full body convulsions. The doctor dropped the syringe and exclaimed those disconcerting words, "Jesus Christ, this kid is dying!"

Everything seemed paradoxically to go into slow motion. He ordered the two guys who had brought me in to hold down my legs, one of the medics to lie across my chest, and the second medic to get a spring loaded syringe of atropine. He injected the medication into my stomach, and I slowly began to calm down.

All of this took place in seconds, but I clearly remember thinking as if it were yesterday,

> *What a non-heroic way to die...I wonder what mom and dad will think...Damn, I didn't get to say good-bye or tell them how much I really loved them.*

A centipede just didn't seem to be very meaningful way to exit planet earth – and so far from home. As it turns out, I was in the hospital for several days with a splitting headache, and survived.

The point of this story is not the preceding event, as attention getting as it was, but rather the impact that it had on the rest of my life. I realized two things from this unexpected pebble dropped into the liquid chemistry of my mind:

One – you can put things in your body over which you have no control – so be very careful about that, and

Two – life is extremely fragile and can be snatched away in no time...completely unpredictably.

It is the second thing I learned that had the biggest effect. When you are young, and particularly when you are a young man in this culture, there is a sense of invulnerability – an almost inherent underlying belief you are indestructible. This event changed that perception in an instant, forever altering my view of life, and as it has played out, the way I interact with others.

Nobody getting up in the morning, with the exception of the condemned or terminally ill, thinks it will be their last day; no child going to school in the morning thinks someone will come into their classroom and take their life before the morning ends; no one getting into their car to head home thinks their life will end within the hour; no person heading to a grocery store to do a little shopping thinks their life will end in the next few minutes or seconds; no one thinks they will never see their mother or father or sister or brother or son or daughter again as the day begins – because, well "…no one thinks the unthinkable…."

Yet this is the uncontrollable nature and randomness of life. There are NO GUARANTEES.

This brush with mortality led to a sea change in the way I looked at life and the lives of those around me. It led to a life-long habit of taking small moments to thank people for their service – colleagues, secretaries, janitors, the waitresses, friends, and family.

The experience led to a life-long habit of looking for ways to compliment people on their work, no matter what their job…a life-long habit of encouraging people in moments of personal struggle…a life-long habit of thanking people for having made a difference in my life…a life long habit of telling people I love that I love and admire them.

The last item is not always easily said nor understood. This is where words often do not work so well. Once you have told someone you love them, the meaning is often left to the understanding of the 'hearer,' rather than that of the 'sayer.' If it is not clear, it can lead to misunderstanding….and surely there are times when I have not had the words to express 'the understanding.' The rewards, however, usually, outweigh the risks.

Some people say this falls under the heading of doing, "…random acts of kindness…" I reject the former and embrace the latter…these acts should never be random, but deliberate 'kindnesses' with gratitude, because "…no one thinks the unthinkable…"

ONWARD AND UPWARD

"The man may teach by doing, and not otherwise. If he can
communicate himself he can teach, but not by words.
He teaches who gives and he learns who receives."
- Emerson

It was 5:00PM on Monday afternoon. He had just topped off his day
seeing patients by lifting weights, as was his custom.

"I'm in Los Angeles seeing patients tomorrow and will be back by
4:30PM. I'll give you a call."

This is the way it always was…We saw each other every day, for the
most part knew each other's schedule, but he would end the day by asking
me what I had planned for the next day, and tell me what was on tap for
him.

Just before we parted, we quietly reminded one another how much we
appreciated finally working together. We did this from time to time, the
way it is important for friends to express how much they mean to one
another, even though they know it in their hearts - words do have meaning.

He slipped the strap of his bag over the left shoulder and gently limped
to the door – a residual gait the result of a stroke he had almost completely
recovered from eight months earlier. He turned and said, with a twinkle in
his eye, as always,

"Onward and Upward!"

His name was Vert. Vert Mooney – now there is a name. Son of Voigt and Naomi originally from Pittsburgh....an orthopedist, the quietest of men, and hardest working person I had ever labored with. While he was trained in the elite institutions of the Eastern establishment, if you didn't know what he did for a living, it would be impossible to guess – his affect was that of the most common of folk.

He and I had known each other for better than 20 years, and had collaborated on any number of projects. We often talked about actually working together, but somehow the stars didn't align themselves until the spring of 2008.

Come West My Friend
I got a call in February of that year. It was that familiar voice, you know the kind...the voice you have heard so many times you can't count, but never tire of. The voice accompanied so often by affirmation and character that when you hear it, it's like putting on those favorite tennis shoes that fit like they had been custom made; the voice that expresses earned respect, love, meaning – the feeling almost always unrelated to the content of the conversation...yeah, you know – 'the voice.'

"Ted, this is Vert." – as if he needed to take those few seconds to identify himself.

He had lost his research coordinator and asked if I might be interested in taking that position.

"Time's slipping away from us, if we don't do it now, we may not get it done at all."

So in June, on the cusp of my sixty-first year, I moved to San Diego, California to be with my friend, my colleague and one of the great human beings I have known.

Habit and Character
If habit leads to character and character to destiny, that would define Vert. When he was home, he was up every morning before five. By five, it was a pot of tea by his side and newspaper in hand. By six, he had devoured both and was off to the shower to get ready for the day. At 6:25 it was breakfast with Ruth his wife; 6:40 in the car and at his desk by 7AM. In his 78th year, this was his routine day in and day out.

His workdays were filled with patients, independent case reviews and writing –Vert surely could write. As a young man, he had taken to the written word. It served him well in later years, and would make him one of the most prolific orthopedic surgeons that ever lived. He published hundreds of scientific papers, wrote book chapters, edited textbooks and added an autobiography to the mix…Yes indeed, Vert could write… His writing would lead to speaking engagements and visiting professor invitations all over the planet.

Emerson said, "…do your work…" and dare to do what you can do best. Doing what you do best is easy to say, but in a world where most of us are confronted with much distraction and the way we appear, rather than the quality of what we do, it is sometimes hard to find what it is that we do best…this was not a problem for my friend Vert.

While his work ethic was impressive, and what he wrote meaningful to the profession he had chosen, it was his example in life that drew me so strongly. He had a willingness to listen to anything, whether he agreed with it or not; his ready mind to reflect what he did know against the forward possibilities of what lay ahead.

Say and do…
There is a great Stephen Sondheim lyric in the Musical "Into the Woods"

Careful the things you say
Children will listen
Careful the things you do
Children will see and learn
Children may not obey, but children will listen
Children will look to you for which way to turn
To learn what to be
Careful before you say "Listen to me"

While these lines are true of children, they are equally true for adults. We look for consistency; we look for examples of strength and faith, and it is here we are inspired to be better tomorrow than we have been today.

What we do is so much more informative than what we say, for it is in the doing we build faith, learn character, understand perseverance, find our mentors, develop self-respect and in the end, slowly get a better understanding of who we are. When what we say matches what we do, that's when it really counts.

The unexpected…

Tuesday afternoon the call came…it was not the 4:30PM call I expected. It was 1:30PM, and it wasn't him calling to say he was home so we could once again arrange for the day that lay ahead, as was so often the case. This call was not about tomorrow, but rather a notification of his unexpected death in a car crash, on his way home from seeing patients in Los Angeles.

"Just before we parted, we quietly reminded one another how much we appreciated finally working together…words do have meaning."

"He turned and said, with a twinkle in his eye, as always, Onward and Upward!"

I was then, and now, grateful for those gentle forward looking words.

They would be our last….

AND THEN THERE WERE TWO

"You might think you want what you see. Be
careful, you may not get what you think..."
- anonymous

We carry two bodies around all the time....

The **physical body** in which we live – programmed to survive some 80
plus years –subject to illness, cold, injury and sometimes, unendurable
agony.

There is, as described in many spiritual writings, the 'us' that lives within
our bodies – sometimes referred to as **the heart or soul** subject also to
pains and troubles of its own.

Both have the capacity, barring accident and proper maintenance, to be
healthy and well. Both clothe themselves – one with cotton, wool or some
other fabric...the other with words, thoughts and ideas. Illness or health,
depend on the way we treat them.

The outside...
Our physical body is subject to certain natural laws, which keep it
running as smoothly as possible. Exercise lubricates and keeps the cobwebs
out, making it able to meet most of the demands of the day. Proper
nutrition – carbohydrate, protein and fat – fuels the engines permitting the
body to do the exercise that loosens and keeps the cobwebs out. Sleep
provides maintenance checks and repairs necessary to use the nutrition that
fuels the engines permitting exercise to...you get the picture.

The thing about the physical side of things is that it is extremely temporary. If not maintained consistently, the system tends to break down. Even when maintained to optimal levels, it slowly wastes away – that we know for certain.

The good news is the early warning systems that keep us apprised of the things that help us remain healthy. If we try to do too much, rapid loss of muscle nutrition and insufficient oxygen reduce our capacity, keeping us from overdoing it. The sensory system tells us if something is too hot, cold, sharp, or too loud. When our fuel gets low, hunger pangs remind us it is time to put some 'gas in the tanks.' If we don't sleep properly we experience fatigue, cognition deficits, balance problems, susceptibility to illness, shortness of temper, and the list goes on.

The thing is that while we describe these systems separately, they all work together like the music of a great symphony – interdependent – each doing its part to create the most awesome of self-actuating systems.

The inside...

Our spiritual body, as described by spiritual writers of Eastern and Western thought, is also subject to certain universal laws, which keep it running as smoothly as possible. It must also be exercised to keep lubricated and the cobwebs out. It exercises faith, hope, love, compassion, trust and many other attributes. It is nourished through the hunger of curiosity and fed with knowledge and understanding. Meditation and prayer provide the maintenance checks and 'rest' that permit renewal needed to exercise the spiritual body in an optimal way.

Like its physical counterpart, these functions work interdependently to create and manifest an even more awe inspiring, self-actuating system.

Things aren't exactly the same

There is, however, a difference between our physical and spiritual bodies. One can be seen and one cannot – yet, both undeniably exist. The fact that no one has ever seen a 'soul,' doesn't mean it (we) doesn't (don't) exist. Thomas Aquinas writes:

"A thing can be self-evident in either of two ways:
on the one hand, self-evident in itself, though not to us;
on the other, self-evident in itself, and to us."
- Summa Theologica

The former argument fits 'us' the soul and the latter, the physical body in which we reside.

Our physical body is evident to itself, and to us, because we can see it; smell it, and touch it. The soul, on the other hand, might be self-evident, but we have never seen one – or ourselves for that matter. Without seeing, smelling or touching the soul, it is not self-evident to us. When we cannot grasp a proof of the existence of something, yet clearly see the effect of the unseen, it becomes accepted as a matter of faith.

Existence of the soul then is a matter of faith.

So what's the point?
This is leading to the way we eat - our hunger and nutrition systems. When we are physically hungry, it is important we eat a properly balanced diet. Sometimes the foods we eat taste good, but are empty calories, meaning there is energy in the food, but not much nutrition (no vitamins or minerals).

Cotton candy is a great example. It looks good, tastes sweet, but one is reminded of comments by Madame Thénardier in Les Miserable (musical) concerning her husband's boasts of manly prowess – "…there's not much there…" Pure carbohydrate in moderation is not a problem, but a steady diet creates difficulties for our metabolism.

The same thing happens spiritually. It is important to eat a properly balanced diet – for example, faith, assurance, love, and compassion to name a few. Sometimes the things we are attracted to seem good, but actually are not satisfactory to us. Our curiosity may be filled with gossip, the news of the day, the tabloid problems of others, the fantasy of the latest film or television show. Surely time occupying, and in moderation, not a problem but very often "…there's not much there…"

It is frequently said, "We are what we eat…" but in fact, "**We eat what we are**." The things we eat are actually the elements our physical bodies are made from…sugars, proteins, fat, a few vitamins and a little water. On the spiritual side, it is my belief that love, joy, peace, gentleness, goodness and faith are elements making up the soul.

Making the choices
Keeping our physical body healthy is a choice…the way we exercise, what we eat, the amount of sleep we get. The quality of activity, food and rest we choose results in the quality of health we have for the years of our journey on this planet.

Keeping our spiritual body healthy is also a choice. In this instance, we become exactly what we choose to be in our lives. No one is responsible for the internal workings of our mind, but us. What we expose ourselves to, what we read, what we watch, what we listen to, what we say, all grow our spiritual body.

So - this day, as we rise to "...do the work of a human being..." let us do it with gratitude and **choose to make this day a better day** for both of our bodies...

HOW CAN THESE THINGS BE?

> "Musical strings, like our spirit, resonate
> with other living beings. Taking a life
> is like cutting that string...
> its resonance forever lost"
> -Anonymous

She was 14 years of age and beaten to death. An accusation was made of adultery, some say rape, but that is incidental.

She was 14 years of age and beaten to death.

While the story captured headlines and caught momentary world attention for its horrific and thoughtlessness, none of it would bring her back. It would soon be forgotten in the moment and life goes on, BUT it would not be momentary nor forgotten in the life of her family – She was 14 years of age and beaten to death.

There is story in the eighth chapter of John of the Bible. A woman is brought to the prophet Christ for his judgment. She was caught in adultery – taken "...in the very act...." The law was clear, adultery was punishable by death...death by stoning, a dreadful way to die. Yet something different happened on this occasion.

Christ was asked by the men who brought her what should be done to this woman. His answer? "He who is without sin, among you, let him first cast a stone...'

The scripture says they were convicted by their conscience and left the scene, the eldest first until they were all gone.

Christ asked the woman, "Where are your accusers?"

There were none. The hearts of these men stung, because they all had had adulterous thoughts. They knew, before God, they could not claim innocence from the very act for which they had accused this woman.

What about this child?

The death of this young girl is tragic, but more so in that it is a metaphor for the kind of thing that is done to women and children victimized all over this world. Murder, rape, humiliation of the weak and helpless is the fare of the more predatory and powerful. One expects to find this in war – not in the name of 'social order,' 'religious custom,' 'family honor,' 'cultural superiority/inferiority,' or in this case 'fatwa.'

> **Fatwa** – *an edict or religious opinion rendered concerning judgment and/or punishment inflicted in the name of God* (what God? whose God?)…or at the very least representing and informal judgment of the **'Shalish'** – *an informal religious court.*

Of course there is no 'personal responsibility' for the punishment and subsequent death of the child…her sentence, after all, was sanctioned. An informal religious court – hmmm. There are far less punitive measure that could have been taken in this matter – and by the way, what about the man, the perpetrator of the vile act that led to this judgment! Reports indicate he was permitted discipline by his family in private and subsequently ran away.

You see, she was 14 years of age and beaten to death.

Our sensibilities are turned upside down by this kind of event. How can this barbaric act be justified, let alone administered by human beings! Were it only an isolated episode, yet one is sickened by any number of atrocities that have been committed and justified for the most singularly selfish of reasons – just because!

One need only look to the history of racial discrimination in this country in the 19th and 20th centuries, to note this is not just the act of a 'barbaric' people - we are not guiltless...

There is no way to recompense for the loss of this child in Bangledesh; there is no way to punish the kind of depravity that led to this unspeakable, deliberate act. What punishment could be meted out that would satisfy the sense of revenge or loss filling the hearts of the parents who whose child is gone?

This, however, isn't just about this little girl or the millions of others that have suffered degradation and oppression…it is about us, and the thoughts we have in *our* minds. What things lurk in the darkness of our hearts that are nurtured and fed? How angered and horrified are we, when contaminated thoughts bubble through our own minds? While we are shocked by what '…those people did to this child…' – are we shocked by the violence, avarice, envy and fear of our internal world.

It is clear there is no action we can personally take in this situation. There is something we can do, however. We can work to ensure within the sphere of our influence that we do not murder and kill with our thoughts and language. We can work to ensure justice within the circle of our control.

We cannot change the way others act and behave unless we are present to the deed, but we can make sure when we find ourselves in situations of judgment, we don't rationalize our actions based on the excuse that it is somebody else's accountability.

We are totally accountable for ourselves for the things over which we have control – as the Greek stoic philosopher Epictitus noted… "the ideas we accept and the opinions we create from them."

She was only 14…

CHILD'S PLAY

> "…Memory! You have the key,
> …Put your shoes at the door…prepare for life."
> - Eliot TS <u>Rhapsody on a Windy Night</u>

You know how it is the seemingly little things that add a certain richness to our lives? The thoughts that bubble up into the stream of consciousness – lost somewhere in the reaches of our memory banks. Lost? Well, in these moments, we appreciate they are not lost, maybe just tucked away somewhere waiting for an opportunity to touch us once again.

I dropped by the community center this week during my morning walk in the park near our home. I was drawn to the gymnasium for a couple of reasons: One, I felt a minor urge for a brief metabolic break and knew there was a bathroom in the building, but more than that, the sound of young kids playing basketball caught my attention…basketball!

Suddenly, I was ten years old and just arriving in Fairmont, West Virginia – the son of a Baptist minister. Our new church had a youth basketball team and Coach Bob, wanting me to feel welcome, invited me to join the team.

There was a small problem – I had never touched a basketball in my life. The inexperience and enthusiasm of youth, however, is seldom deterred by such detail.

Let the games begin

In the arena of youth church basketball; in those days, kids didn't practice…they played. It was in the crucible of play one gained experience. I found myself on a team, and in a shirt with the church name written in big letters across the chest…a chest, I might add that seemed just a little bigger for having my own shirt. I was a small kid, with a yet unknown and quite unexpected growth spurt lying a year or two ahead.

The gym at the Episcopal Church was conveniently located just across the street from my dad's church. We had been in town about a week when that Saturday morning came, with a bright sun and the excitement of this new game - basketball.

Coach Bob was a real motivator and had the entire team excited about the game against those Methodists. None of the kids had met me yet, so introductions were made and I was given that wary look – you know, the kind that says, "Who are you, and what are you doing here?"

The game began and it was exciting - parents lined the wall in the tiny gym cheering for their children and teams.

Coach Bob, couldn't exactly put me in as a starter, even if I was the preacher's kid. He waited until everyone else had played a little.

Preparation...what's the point?
Then came 'the look' and 'the call' – "Ted, go in for Billy!" I can't remember being more excited in my life, nor as it turned out, could I have been less prepared. The other team scored; a teammate took the ball out and tossed it to me. Tucking the ball under my arm, I ran down the court. It was clear sailing because everybody seemed to be standing still. A whistle blew, but I was undeterred…approaching the basket I took the ball with both hands and threw it with all the enthusiasm I could muster.

Two immediate problems and one circumstance resulted.

The problems: one doesn't tuck the ball under their arm and run down the court without dribbling, AND the idea is to put the ball **in the basket** – I missed the entire banking board!

The circumstance: Coach Bob pulled me out of the game after that one 'run and shoot,' and I never played again the rest of the season. Coach Bob was disappointed because he was hoping he had a new ball player, I was disheartened because it seemed there was no future in a game, for all my youthful enthusiasm, I didn't understand.

It has been said, "Anything worth doing is worth doing POORLY…UNTIL you have enough experience to do it well!"

That is the good news! There is a resiliency in youth – an unspoken "…hope springs eternal…" that keeps a child motivated. You know, the standing and falling that happens again and again UNTIL standing becomes second nature. It is one of the greatly intimate experiences of life to watch a child succeed in its unrelenting desire to stand and walk.

It is the alphabet, not the novel that starts the game...
You think seemingly small moments don't mean anything?

I would be 12 years old as a second/third string player on a junior high basketball team, before I would make my first shot in a game. It was against St. Peter's Junior High and the guy guarding me was Mike Glendenning. While that shot was the smallest of things to my team members or the outcome of that game – making <u>that</u> shot against <u>that</u> boy inspired me to continue to play a game I later learned to love.

How meaningful was that shot? I am 63 years old at the moment, and still remember the name of the guy over whom I made those two points! That shot – those two points were enough to carry me through subsequent years in a game that taught me the life lessons of self-discipline, fair play, the transience of defeat and great joys of success. Those two points carried me through hours in the schoolyard shooting, shooting and shooting some more. **Those two points? They were priceless!!**

Lessons for old(er) folk...
There are those times, when from somewhere deep inside a voice comes that says, "…keep it up…this was a success…this moment has meaning…" These are the quiet times…they don't come in large and loud voices, but they are electric. This is when the 'still small voice' reminds us that we have worth and meaning.

When memories like this find their way to the surface of my consciousness, I try to take a few moments to immerse myself in them and feel gratitude, because they remind me that success comes from hard work; that truly one reaps what one sows. Equally important, as we get older, there is a tendency to dwell on what we haven't done or what we can't do - the young are not plagued by this. It is instructive to remember those success moments when they appear.

I am willing to bet each of you has a 'Mike Glendenning' moment(s) tucked away somewhere in the depths of your life experience that have come at just the right time and in just the right way – the moment that gave you confidence to continue to '...play the game...' and the hope that tomorrow would be a better day.

These thoughts do not come by accident, nor should they be lightly dismissed. They might be just the touch needed in the busy course of life – the '...two points...' scored, as it were, to help carry through a difficult circumstance or event - the quiet touch for just a little more hope.

It is said we are creatures of spirit moving through life in physical bodies. I believe this, because it is often the physical experiences in our lives that contribute to our spiritual well being. I am guessing this working relationship (spirit/body), has a broader and more purposeful meaning...

Thanks Mike...wherever you are.

HOW ABOUT THOSE HANDS?

"It's in the little things that life is made…
the smile, the touch, the kindness.
From the little become the great, and
greatness lies in these small acts."
- Anonymous

Have you noticed it is the small things that so often make a difference? A knowing glance, a quiet nod of affirmation, a kind word, a polite gesture or a gentle touch – the little things that shape our life experience. It's said when people know each other well; "…a smile is better than a word, a wink than a smile, and a nod than a wink,"

But the touch…ah the touch…now there is something…little is more powerful than the human touch! Maybe that's why we have so many delicate sensory receptors in our fingers. Touch protects us from too much heat, cold, things that are too sharp, and permits us to sense the correct pressure to firmly shake a person's hand or gently pick up a fragile egg.

Of the primary senses of the fingers, pressure has the most receptors. Take a moment to brush your thumb gently across your fingertips noticing the pressure and sensation. Then run the fingers of one hand lightly down the palm side fingers of the other hand – note the difference between the two activities. Now close your eyes and softly touch your face – forehead, cheeks, eyebrows, lips and nose – sense the differences in texture.

Touch…what a gift!

While touch does have a 'reporting function' – heat, cold, pressure and pain – it is NOT just the colliding of electrons from skin to skin, or skin to object, that brings the real magic to this sensory phenomenon. There is much more than meets 'the touch' as it were.

Touching another person, for example, can be a wondrous sensory experience. There is little doubt the one touching and the one receiving, both feel a sense of heightened connection. It's hard to find something more satisfying and sometimes more intimate than the loving caress from the hand one person to another.

More than a physical phenomenon
In the scriptures, Christ finds himself amongst a large crowd of people. He says to his disciples,

"Who touched me?"

One of them, with a '...*you have got to be kidding me...*' expression replies, "...there is a crowd of people around you – bumping, pushing – and you are asking who touched you!"

Jesus responds, "...**somebody** hath **touched me**: for I perceive that virtue is gone out of me..." (Luke 8:46)

A lot of people were touching Christ physically, but *someone* had *touched him spiritually* AND taken something from him – a transfer of spirit from Christ's spiritual body to a woman and she was healed.

It is a spiritual thing
It could be argued that fingers and touch are a metaphor for something deeper – a channel of communication – a conduit whereby spirit is transferred from one person to another. It slips through the skin, muscle, bone, and **reaches the soul**. Touch transcends the physical – it really is spiritual in every way.

Sometimes when we hear Biblical and other miraculous reports that happen to people, we think of it as strange; it even makes some people a little uncomfortable. In a real sense, it is about the laying on of hands. This isn't something limited to the realm of spirit filled Pentecostal or Evangelical people....we all do it every day in the most common of ways – a shake of the hand, a pat on the back, or a 'high-five.'

Everybody '...lays on hands...'
Most all parents tell stories of how a distraught child was calmed when

taken in their arms. This was simply transferring peace or assurance from parent to child through the laying on of hands. A soothing word of course helps, but it is the touch that counts.

As adults, we all identify with times when we were fortified by a pat on the arm or a brief hug in a moment of need. It doesn't even have to be a moment of need. Maybe it's just the greeting to a friend or family member. It is just nice to receive an affirmation by human contact that comes in this way.

Athletes understand how important a thoughtful slap on the shoulder, from a teammate or coach, returns the spirit of confidence for their game.

It is instinctive that we reach out to touch those who find themselves in need – even more so toward those with whom we have a bond – those we love and care about.

A pair of docs!
The paradox of modern society is that we have been provided so many things intended to make the quality our lives better. Computers do a lot of work previously done by hand, cell phones allow us to talk from practically anywhere, and texting messages can keep us in instantaneous contact with short bursts of information.

In an unfortunate way, these labor saving devices have allowed us to better communicate information, but do not provide the kind of spiritual exchange we get from that profoundly subtle and sometimes not so subtle gesture of physical/spiritual human contact.

Sometimes less is more; being physically present with others is much more helpful than a call or text. In spite of this kind of communication being fairly recent, it is instructive to note that even the ancients appreciated the importance of the bond of the universal human family. My friend Mark says,

> "Consider often the connection of all things in the Cosmos and their relationship with each other. For in a way all things are actually intertwined, and thus according to this there is a natural inclination, or love that links everything together..."
>
> - Aurelius M <u>Meditations</u>

For all the ways we communicate, without being present with one another, there is nothing like touch to engage our senses when we are together. This is our nature! Withholding sensory communication from one another is against the nature we have been given.

Remember the touch…it's the little things – they are huge!

IT'S ALL IN THE VOICE

"…with so much that has been given,
what is our obligation?"
- Anonymous

"Samuel, Samuel, " the voice called…

The ritual was the same most nights. There would be a hug and a kiss good night, proceeded by a short prayer thanking God for the day and for those who might be less fortunate than us.

Then there would be those special nights – there were many as a child, when Mum told me stories. Her favorites, and by extension mine, were those of the Old Testament in the Bible. One I loved to hear, and would request from time to time, was about Samuel.

The tale…
A fellow named Elkanah (El-cain-ah) had two wives: Hannah and Peninah. Peninah (Pe-nee-nah) produced several children, but Hannah was barren…and pretty depressed about it. One year, quietly and bitterly praying to God, she negotiated:

"…If, thou wilt look on the affliction of thine handmaid, and **remember me**, and not forget thine handmaid, but wilt give unto thine handmaid a man child, then I will give him unto the Lord all the days of his life…" (1 Samuel 1:11 – <u>Bible</u>)

The deal? Give me a boy and I'll give him back to you.

128

She returned home, and the scripture says, "...Elkanah knew Hannah his wife; **and the Lord remembered her**." Thus begins the unlikely journey of Samuel, one of the pivotal characters of the Old Testament.

When the child was two, Hannah took him to the Priest Eli and gave him to the old man. This was her deal...give me the child and I'll give him back - she honored the arrangement. Somewhere around the age of five, Samuel was sleeping and God called him.

The scripture says, "...the Lord called Samuel...," but my mother recounted that God said, "Samuel, Samuel..." There is no way for me to express the quiet and urgent gentleness of my mother's voice as she spoke those words, but in the imagination of a young child, I was transported to the very room where God spoke to this little boy.

Samuel thought it was the old priest calling him and went to see what he wanted. The priest, of course had not done so. This was repeated twice before the Eli realized God was trying to communicate with the boy. He instructed Samuel to say, "...Speak Lord; for thy servant heareth..." – which Samuel did, ultimately leading to Samuel's role in the birth the Hebrew monarchy.

This was just one of many stories Mum recounted to her little boy. They were intimate and animated and full of quiet enthusiasm. You see, I was Samuel to my mother. It is not that she was barren, for I was given two sisters. It is that she had fervently prayed that God would give her children, that she and my father could care for, and raise with purpose.

Mum explained to me - maybe it was when I first heard the story of Samuel - I didn't belong to her and my dad. I was a gift from God and it was their obligation and duty to raise me for Him. It is difficult to express the comfort of these words from her. There was the sense that this was a team effort...*inclusive – not exclusive*.

She and dad had conceived me, but in fact, I was to be a free moral agent, in the process being prepared to hear 'the voice' myself. That was their job as she saw it. Teach me the language, tell me the stories, inform me of my place in this world and then turn me loose - her work complete.

She said to me, "Teddy, it might not come as clearly as "Samuel, Samuel...,"" but it would come. The task might not be of Samuel's magnitude, but...*it would be*. I should be aware, she continued, that like Samuel, it might take time to recognize God's leading, but if I kept my mind open, I would eventually recognize 'the voice.'

And so my childhood would go. Mum was clever when telling many of these stories, taking poetic license here and there. Some of the Biblical stories are fairly explicit, if not in language, certainly in intent.

The story of Esther provides an example. A King named Ahasurerus (A-hash-U-E-rus), had divorced his wife and was looking for a new queen. His counselors rounded up the young virgins of the kingdom, prepared them and presented them, one per night. Esther was one of these girls. He took a great affection to her and made her his queen. Mum explained the reason the king liked Esther so much was that she was a "...very good story teller, and the king really enjoyed them."

As the years have gone by, some of the warmest memories I have are the times I had with my mother in the twilight of the day – telling me stories. As she encouraged, I have tried to listen for 'the voice' as my journey has unfolded. As anyone that seeks knows, discerning God's leading is not always evident. Yet, seekers know 'the sound' *when* they hear it. It may not be clear to others what the voice of God sounds like, but I can assure you, when He quietly speaks to my heart, it is the distinct and quiet voice of my mother calling "Ted, Ted..."

NOBODY DOES IT ALONE

"Who can say if I've been changed for the better
But because I knew you I have been changed for good"
- Elphaba: <u>Wicked</u> the Musical

"I gotta go."

"Where do you want to go?" She said.

In his own private world, anxiously moving around the porch, he replied, "I gotta go."

Different words this time around…different feelings this time around…There was so much to say, yet no place for it to be said.

The beginning, as all stories should start…

Jim was head football coach for the biggest rival school in our town. Fairmont was, at that time, about ten thousand hearty souls in the middle of the soft, bituminous coal fields of West Virginia. While Jim coached '…the other guys for the competing team…', his daughter went to my high school. He always seemed friendly, and while his daughter and I were not an item, I was kind of sweet on her.

We had come to Fairmont in the late 1950s, to a new church…a new town…a different culture for Canadian expatriates. From the fifth grade through high school and to college, this was my home. It was here friendships were formed; the life and voice changing discomfort of puberty, and the social revolution of the late 1960s. It all happened in this small town nestled on the banks of the Monongahela River in the West Virginia hills.

After high school, I went on to university, but was not successful. The Vietnam War was on, and I was drafted. Like other young foreigners with immigrant status and a 'green card,' military service became an unexpected reality. Those years I spent as an Air Traffic Controller for Uncle Sam.

The years passed…

After separating from the Army, I returned to Canada, to live with my mother's sister. Because I was not an American Citizen, I could not ply my military air traffic control training and experience in the United States. I stayed with my aunt while making application to the Canadian Department of Transport to manage aircraft in the land of my birth. Passing the tests and physical was not a problem; I was young, healthy and had already controlled air traffic in one of the least known, and busiest airports in the world – Vung Tau Army Airfield in the Republic of South Vietnam.

After notice of acceptance, there was a month or so before the training program began and I headed to West Virginia to see a few folk. Life had moved on and the 'Coach' was now 'Dr.'…teaching at the local college. On a whim, I stopped by to visit with him for a couple of reasons: 1) – to see how he liked teaching at the college level, and 2) – to see the status of his daughter.

We chatted for only a few minutes, but in that short time – in those few words – the course of my life was about to change in a completely inconceivable way. He asked if I had finished school…the answer a "no." I wouldn't need a degree to control air traffic. It was a good profession, and work I really enjoyed.

He suggested, taking a year to finish school. A degree would be a good idea…after all; one might never know when having a diploma might come in handy. He argued that time would pass no matter what I was doing, and that finishing school would be a small thing, with no real downside – his words…"I'm not saying you should return to school, I'm just saying you should take it under consideration."

Money in the bank of life…

This was a man who understood people. In particular, he understood young men. He understood one guides, one doesn't mandate. He understood, motivation must come from within. The key? Find the 'sweet spot' in the young person's mind, and let them think it was 'their idea.' He understood, that 'life example' in addition to edifying 'words,' builds currency in the bank of human relationships…he had invested wisely and was a man with plenty of capital in the lives of others.

I'm not sure about the events that occurred over the next three or four days, but by the end of that week, I had contacted the Department of Transport in Canada – requested and received a year's delay for the start date in ATC school – and was enrolled in Fairmont State College! I never did return to Canada to move those airplanes around the sky. That brief encounter caused a 'sea change' in my life.

During that final year or so in Fairmont, Jim became for me what he had been for hundreds of young men in his career – a quiet but solid place of solace and comfort when the storms of life seemed too much. He was a man who appeared to take comfort in watching 'his boys' grow into men.

After leaving Fairmont, the journey led to LaCrosse, Wisconsin for graduate work, finally the University of Missouri for completion of formal post-graduate education. The smell of jet fuel and crowded airspace seemed a distant and increasingly fading memory.

The unbroken thread…
Once or twice over the years, I headed back to Fairmont with only one driving goal in mind…to see Jim. I wanted to remind him again, the investment of his time and attention had been meaningful and worthwhile; I wanted to remind him he had changed my life, and was part of every success I had; I wanted to remind him, while people I met over the years never knew him…everyone of them felt a piece of him in my words and spirit; I wanted to remind him I loved him and appreciated the immeasurable influence he had had on my life.

He would always seem a bit surprised at the intensity and enthusiasm with which I shared my adventures, always finishing with gratitude for his influence…he almost seemed embarrassed by my words. You see, he was simply doing the job for which God had called him. He was following the leading that had been put in his heart. He wasn't thinking about what any of it might mean…he was just doing his job. His quiet, but steady enthusiasm for life was so palpable; you wanted to be a part of it.

With an irregular regularity, I would write, catching him up on the events of my life – a note coming back with a 'congratulations' and brief thanks.

A couple of years ago I wrote and nothing came. A month or so later I received a letter from his wife. It sat on my desk for a week – I was afraid to open it. I didn't want to face the news that his journey was over.

Finally, when I could avoid it no longer, I steeled myself and opened the letter. Jim was not dead, it was worse...he had Alzheimer's disease. I was overwhelmed.

A journey home...

I knew I was going to be in Fairmont for a reunion the next year and asked his wife whether I might come by and see him. She said, "sure," and on a warm summer's day, in those West Virginia hills, I was honored to spend time with this gentle man who had changed everything about my life.

I wanted, yet once again, to tell him how much he had and still meant; I wanted to say, yet once again, how grateful I was that he had given me the option to 'think' and 'do' something better with my life. I wanted him to tell me that he loved me too, and that he had always known my life had purpose.

I did say some of those things...but there is hollowness when there are no receptors on the other end...an emptiness when words are spoken out of season, when "...the salt has lost its savor."

I longed to hear him say, "I'm not saying you should, I'm just saying you should take it under consideration." Instead, he puttered anxiously around the porch of his home repeating: "I gotta go...I gotta go"

I am reminded how important it is to let people you care about know that you do. I have learned to do it at the moment the thought occurs...not waiting until some time in the future. I have learned how important it is...Not just for their sake, but for my own...

I'm not saying you should tell people who have touched your life, that you care about and love them; I'm just saying you should "...take it under consideration..."

LOVE COVERS A MULTITUDE OF SINS

> And Adam knew Eve his wife,
> and she conceived, and bare Cain,
> and said, I have gotten a man from the LORD.
> Genesis 4:1 – <u>Bible</u>

I lied to her once...

There were sins of omission, but the lie...that lie was so traumatic... thinking about it 46 years later still brings some discomfort!

The background

Fannie Margaret Maude Arnott was her name. By the time I understood that she had any name at all she had acquired one more - ' Dreisinger'. Yes, Fanny Margaret Maude Arnott was my mother, but I didn't even know that. It took months before I could even say "...mama...," the oft repeated word she used when appearing in my field of vision. She was a real "coo-er", and a quiet singer of lullabies. A gentle soul and like so many mothers, was sure her baby boy was something special!

In some ways, she was ill equipped to mother a boy. Married in her 30th year, she had not been around many boys, other than her three brothers...being a 'tom-boy' didn't really qualify. She had gone to a school where there were no boys; became a school teacher and - before marrying Edward James - taught during the school year, traveled with her girlfriends and worked summers as a counselor at a girl's camp in the Laurentian Mountains of Quebec.

She was an active athlete as a girl and young woman. She could ride horses, snow ski, play basketball with the best of them, ice skate and win league championships on the tennis courts. While a good sport, she was a formidable and tenacious opponent, who taught her children to play hard...and play fair. Winning was not necessary for character growth - best effort was. In life, it was the end game that counted – the smaller events provided the building blocks for character, and winning was not always the best teacher.

She admonished her kids to...finish the whole race...be the tortoise if necessary...the little engine that could...the person left standing "at the end of the day." Consistency and hard work were the keys. There was just something about that woman - she was special!

By the time I arrived on the planet, she had a decade and thousands of hours of preparation for my entrance into the fray. It would be different for her to teach a boy, but a born teacher she was. She would bravely say it was really only a difference in plumbing, wasn't it?

She taught me almost everything physical in my childhood and early youth from her wealth of experience...play, swim, canoe, water ski, basketball and how to run.

She taught me almost everything spiritual...story after story about brave men and women of the scriptures. She taught me almost everything about the coming challenges of life with morality story after morality story from Aesop to Hans Christian Anderson, to the Little Engine that Could.

She loved music and taught all of us to sing, "...just find a harmony..." she would say and then sing some more. She taught me about gentleness and respect for women, an unrelenting theme from my earliest remembrances through my high school years.

"Think of other girls," she would say, "as though they are your sisters or me."

As a youngster, I have to admit, the sisters' part didn't always inspire thoughts of gentleness!!

The event terrible

The date was October 13, 1967. It is easy to remember because it was her birthday, and the day I learned a life lesson that both informed the rest of my life, and still haunts me.

It was Morgantown, West Virginia - home of 'The Mountaineers.' For some reason she had come by on her way back to Ohio from a churchwomen's conference at Alderson-Broaddus College in Phippi - a small town tucked away in the West Central Allegheny Mountains of that mountainous state. By now she and my father lived in Canton, Ohio, but Mum continued her ties with the churchwomen with whom she had built strong spiritual ties. She left the conference early in the day and surprised me. She loved surprises. We had breakfast together before her 140-mile drive home.

I had forgotten it was her birthday until about half way through breakfast. Not wanting her to realize it had gotten away from me, I told her I had a gift, but had given it to my sister who was also in school at the University. I said it wasn't a problem because I would be coming home on the weekend and would bring it with me. We hugged and kissed good-bye; she headed home, and I to classes for the day.

It was around 4:30 that afternoon when I received a phone call from my sister...an agitated sister! What was this about a birthday present she was supposed to have for mother??? My brain went numb!

The 'worst' laid plans..

Fannie Margaret Maude Arnott Dreisinger "...aka Mum..." had NOT driven home after breakfast, but spent the entire day tracking my sister down to pick up the 'phantom' birthday present, not because she couldn't wait for the surprise, but because she thought it would make it easier for me coming home on the weekend. She wouldn't have opened it anyway, it wasn't in her character to not share the moment with giver of the gift...the giver of the gift...the liar with NO gift.

There were parallel surprises that day. My mother's disappointment causing some damage to her trust levels with me, AND to me for having been caught in so blatant and foolishly constructed betrayal of that woman's trust. She would have been satisfied with a "Happy Birthday Mum," and "I'll see you on the weekend." BUT I had created a castle of sand and it didn't take much of a wind to blow it away.

Facing the music

Mothers have some unknown and mysterious gift of forgiveness. I would have preferred a slow death of 10,000 cuts then to have faced my mother that weekend...but face her I did.

She didn't chastise me for my deceit; she didn't question how I could have so callously disrespected her; she didn't complain she had spent an entire day chasing the wind...she did worse! She told me how she loved me and how open her heart was to me; she quietly and gently said she hoped it would never happen again, and thought it to be a good learning experience....

AND THEN, Fannie Margaret Maude Arnott Dreisinger did what was the 'hallmark of her character,' **she never spoke of it again**. The effect this event had on that tender-hearted soul, I never really knew, but I know what effect it had on me...I was 'cut to the quick' and I never lied nor misled her again as long as that woman lived.

> "Humpty Dumpty sat on the wall
> Humpty Dumpty had a great fall
> All the king's horses and all the king's men
> Couldn't put Humpty Dumpty together again."
> - Mother Gooses' Melodies

The lesson

While the fall with Mum was not fatal, it was a stumble in the long-distance run of life. But as my mother was fond of saying it is not the wins from which we learn the most from...it's the defeats.

In the waning years of her life, she didn't know who I was. She seemed to know I was familiar and loved to have her hair and face stroked. The times we spent together in those last years always made me think of how much of her I carry with me and that life lessons come with a price....

MARKING TIME

> "Life's race-course is fixed; Nature has only a single path and
> that path is run but once, and to each stage of existence has
> been allotted its own appropriate quality; so that the weakness of
> childhood, the impetuosity of youth, the seriousness of middle life,
> the maturity of old age – each bears some of Nature's fruit,
> which must be garnered in its own season."
> Cicero – <u>On Old Age</u>

Yesterday I got older. "Older than what," one might ask? It wasn't a special day, not some accelerant that speeds the burning fire of life…It was merely a day…But in that day, I got older.

Intro – take one

"Hi I'm Dr. Brown," she said. And so she was. Young, tiny, dressed as if she were going out to dinner – it was only 10AM! It is odd when the physician attending to your needs looks like, well the '…every girl (boy)…' in any high school…anywhere. That immediate impression was quickly overcome by doing the math and appreciating undergraduate school, medical school, an internship, a residency, and if she had been in practice any length of time, by now she would be in her early to mid thirties!

This was one of those unrequested markers in life…it is not that they are turning doctors out earlier and younger, but that I am getting older…well, how about more mature. And by the way, what is that invisible line one crosses entering the category of 'older age?' What is the metric? Plato says, "Or suppose we differ in magnitudes, do we not quickly end the difference by measuring?" Well, there is no measurement here so it is difficult to quantify this aging thing!

I have heard it frequently said, "…you are as young (old) as you feel…," but in my experience it is most often said by young folks to older folks complaining about how quickly time has flown by!!!

In an attempt to 'keep my youth,' I have tried to be moderately careful about what I eat, exercise regularly and get a good night's sleep. The latter has not been consistently as good as I would like. Hypnos (the Greek God of sleep) seems to have been inconsistent in his responsibilities in recent months....but I digress.

Intro – take two...

"Hi, I'm Dr. Brown," she said.

"Hi, I'm Ted."

I had been sitting in the chair in her exam room for about 20 minutes waiting for my eyes to dilate.

I had been noticing for some time my right eye seemed to 'feel' like it was working a little harder than my left. Gone for almost two decades was a 'glasses-free life,' with the emergence of a small astigmatism in that pesky right eye. A week ago, there had been an unusual 'floater' in that eye and some small 'lightening flashes' in its periphery. So, thinking there might be a retinal issue, it was off to the Ophthalmologist.

This brings us up to date.

Intro – take three

"Hi, I'm Dr. Brown," she said, and went about shining bright lights in my openly and vulnerably dilated eyes. It was lots of, "look up – look down – look right – look left."

After a few moments she said, "You have some macular pucker (epiretinal membrane) in that right eye."

"When some people get older, the vitreous fluid of the eye contracts and pulls a bit of the membrane away from the back of the lens and wrinkles, kind of like cellophane. Once it happens, it usually doesn't get worse. It can be removed surgically with tiny instruments, but there can be significant complications for some people, and no guarantees. I am happy to refer you to an opthamalic surgeon, because I don't operate."

Hmm, I thought...I come reporting a minor distraction to my right eye; am given no treatment other than a possible, but not probable surgical solution with a 50/50 possibility of success; 6 month healing time, and oh yes – I later checked the internet – much worse...the possibility of blindness in that eye.

"Well," said I, "I am more inclined to let the natural history unfold than have surgery, but thanks."

"Okay," she replied. "I have to say, I am surprised you are seeing as well as you are with this. Your prescription is fine, come see me in a year."

A little reflection

It's easy to not pay too much attention to life as time moves forward. The morning comes...we meet it and get on with the day, as if we have an unlimited number of these 24-hour cycles. The truth, of course, is that we actually have precious few of them.

They fly by with such speed we hardly notice...until...until we have those moments that remind us we are no longer the boys and girls of summer; remind us how good the early spring was; remind us of the richness of the fall harvest...and overcome us with how chilly the winter can be.

Bodily systems break down...it's just what happens and is nothing more than time and gravity doing their jobs. It's just that we, in the ebb and flow of our lives, have few markers to tell us how the journey is actually going or how successful and meaningful all of it is.

Our dance was done

And so it was. She was out the door to the next patient and I was out the door to...well, I was out the door with a label, an unresolvable contracted vitreous fluid – the result of time, gravity, and the natural aging process...emphasis 'aging' – and the rest of the day.

Intro – part four

"Hi, I'm Dr. Brown," she said. I replied, "Hi I'm Ted."

"I am older today...."

THINGS ARE NEVER QUITE THE SAME

"The whispered conversations in overcrowded hallways
The atmosphere as thrilling here as always...
Why, everything's as if we never said goodbye"
- Norma Desmond in
Webber, AL: <u>Sunset Boulevard</u>

He couldn't keep up no matter how hard he tried, yet try he did. She burst away from him to see her son...while he shuffled along the best that he could.

The war for me was over...time in-service in that foreign land done...debt paid...life spared and back to all things familiar...if indeed things are ever truly familiar.

How this started

When I received orders for Vietnam, I reported to a base on the West Coast where I was housed with a lot of other young men headed for the same destination, in a large building full of bunk beds. "Housed" might not exactly be exactly correct. There is no doubt we were under roof, but there were military police at the exits, and we were...well, we were not permitted to leave until we shipped out. This was a precautionary tale of little doubt...a concern that some of the soldiers would slip out and go AWOL...away without leave!

A little family context...

My father had been a proponent of the war. Communism was the great enemy, and if Vietnam fell – as the domino theory went – it would then be all of Southeast Asia. I can recall many conversations and discussions he had with any number of people regarding how important it was for democracy to stop communism in the Republic of Vietnam (the South)...from Ho Chi Minh and the puppet masters in Moscow (the north). They were, of course, the real villains.

It is said, "...it is much easier to tell someone how to dig the ditch than it is to dig it yourself..." My Dad, like so many Americans at the time, had no real skin in the game. He was far removed from the oppressive heat and horror that was the Vietnam war.

No skin...far removed...UNTIL his son – his ONLY son was drafted and was about to be sent to that far away land, where even the modest living of a minister of the Gospel was palatial, compared to the third world living conditions of Southeast Asia.

The change in my father's politic wasn't dramatic or quick, but if you paid attention, there was a clear shift and adaptation in his thought process. He was less apt to get into discussions about the war as you could see him confronted with the very real possibility he would lose his son and namesake.

He was a passionate, but guarded man, who metered out his feelings in the context of the Gospel of Jesus Christ. He was careful to protect the temper he had grown up with and other testosterone driven instincts with which all men struggle. The war had come home to roost on his doorstep, and ate away at him as he struggled mightily to keep it all in. He worked hard to act above the fray, but he labored over my impending departure...he lost sleep, and in quiet moments, he wept.

Harboring powerful feelings take their toll on all of us. My profession, in later years, provided an understanding of the devastating effect unchecked circulating hormones can have on the body...how mental stresses emerge in the most profound of ways, as the internal chemistry turns on itself, attacking the weaker ramparts first; once they are undermined, they challenge the next vulnerable spot, and the next, and the next...

Yet fathers are often bigger than life and so with the stiffest of upper lips my Mother and he hugged and kissed their only boy good-bye, bidding him that he fare well in this unknown and dangerous journey.

There were no, "Go make the world a safer place for democracy"...no,

"Whatever happens, be honorable"…no, "You are making an unselfish sacrifice for your country and family"…there was rather what had always been our custom – a small family circle, as he prayed to the God of Abraham, Isaac and Jacob to keep me safely in His hands.

Off to see the wizard…

There isn't much in the memory banks about that brief stay out West, but soon I was "…leaving on a jet plane…" with a lot of other young men headed so far West, we arrived in the East…the Far East! All of us were in clean and newly issued jungle fatigues, wide-eyed with no, and I mean NO idea what lay ahead.

After a stop at Clark Airbase in the Philippines, and Okinawa (due to some engine trouble), we touched down late in the evening at Ton Son Nhut air base in Saigon – today, Ho Chi Minh City. There was no jet-way from which to depart the plane, just a staircase sitting in an alien land with the immediacy of a crushing humidity, and a kind of indescribable odor…not a bad odor, just different from the West Virginia hills from which I had come and to which I had been accustomed.

The aircraft did not shut down its engines, for its crew had "…promises to keep, and miles to go before [they slept]…". The shorter their time on the ground in a war zone, the better they liked it. After all, they were just ferrying a new batch of 'virgin' soldier boys…in-country, and an equal number of 'not so virgin' young soldier men waiting for the same stairway…out of country. These were not freshly showered GIs in clean uniforms…they looked worn and tired in the damp, dark, moonless and dimly lit tarmac.

As we marched by them, at what was our beginning and their end, there were cat-calls and more than a few comments about how we might not make the 'going home' line in 13 months…mildly entertaining to them…disconcerting to us.

Suddenly, we were there and they were not. In what seemed the blink of an eye, the plane was reloaded, back in the air – the sound of the jet diminishing in the distance like the last ferry to the mainland, escaping the impending storm. They were leaving us to…leaving us to…well, just leaving us.

The year was, as one might say, what it was. Adventures unknown presented themselves; memories created…many remembered…some buried never to be repeated.

It was time to leave

Thirteen months practically to the day, I found myself standing in line with a number of tired and worn soldiers, on the tarmac Ton Son Nhut airfield in Saigon waiting for another "…jet plane…" to land. This aircraft carried the exact number of arriving soldiers, but now we were waiting to get on, get out and go home. The only thought, "Let's get on that plane and out of the airspace before anything happens." A free floating anxiety wandering through my mind, that after an unpredictable year, something might actually happen at the last minute, preventing us from flying so far East, we would reach the safety of the West!

The flight home took me to the West Coast, then to Dover Army airfield on the East Coast, where I picked up a domestic flight to Ohio, where my parents were living. By then I had called to let Mum and Dad know I was safe and the time of arrival.

'Familiarity' doesn't mean 'the same'

What I didn't know in the year I was away, was that my father had Parkinson's Disease, and by now could no longer conceal its symptoms, slowly encroaching on his body and his life…that my father worried and ached for my safety every single day…that he would become progressively infirmed, until this disease completely debilitated him…prematurely ending his life.

As the aircraft approached the regional airport in Canton, Ohio, everything slowed down. It seemed the plane could not get to the ground fast enough. When it did, I entered the terminal yearning to touch them, and at the same time wondering whether I would seem different to them.

In those days, waiting people could come right to the gate. There they were, in the distance coming my way. She saw me and ran with all she had in her. "He couldn't keep up as hard as he tried, and try he did. She burst away from him to see her son…," to touch his hair, to kiss his face, to be assured that it was really him and not the frequently recurrent dream that he was safely home. He couldn't keep up as she left his side and "…shuffled along the best he could…," because by now the Parkinson's in full bloom.

In spite of the excitement of the moment, I was stunned to see this invincible man, this bigger than life personality, struggling to move – for that is the curse of Parkinson's; the difficulty of voluntary movement. As we embraced, holding fast in each other's arms, I could feel the tremors and toll this disease had taken from him in a little over a year.

Yet the prayer had been answered. I had fared reasonably well and the God of Abraham, Isaac and Jacob had kept me in His hand. More importantly, in spite of my father's infirmity, and the unspoken drain on my mother's life, we were together safely in one another's arms.

We were not the same people who had prayed together and said good-bye. As it turns out, we had all been at war that year...all of us had lost a little something. And yet, words cannot express the feelings of that moment...the strength of love, and the ability to nurture and protect that love, even in the most strenuous of absences.

In that moment, whatever had happened in that year meant nothing, for we had the most coveted gift any human being can ask for...each other.

WE STILL HAD EACH OTHER

> I am not so much delighted by my reputation for
> Wisdom…as I am by the hope that the memory
> of our friendship will always endure."
> - Cicero, MT: <u>On Friendship</u>

I have met few people I disliked from the beginning, but Bob was one of the few. I had finished basic training and after taking a leave, was assigned to Air Traffic Control (ATC) School in Biloxi, Mississippi. The U.S. Army was an odd place for an expatriate Canadian – Green Card holding – private first class to find himself, but find myself there I did. The Army did not have a training program for air traffic controllers, so we were sent to Keesler Air Force Base in Biloxi…my first real exposure to the deep south, and Biloxi was about as deep as you could get.

The airbase was near the junction of highway 15 and coastal highway 90…its main gate some 2000 feet (400 meters) from the Gulf of Mexico. We were a small contingent on a compound of about 10 wooden, two story open-bay barracks, and a command building at the northwest end. The middle of the area was open, mostly the kind of shallow sandy gravel with small patches of grass so common to coastal regions of the South.

While it was wartime, or rather military conflict time, there were only so many instructors in the school. We trained along side Air Force boys, which meant we had to wait until a slot opened up to start training. Integrating into the system took time…sometimes several weeks or more, in that sultry, hot, humid late summer weather common to the Gulf Coast region of the country.

What to do...

What do you do with a group of testosterone filled young men in their late teens and early twenties with a little too much time on their hands? I'm not sure what other organizations do, but the military 'makes work' to keep you busy. Policing the yard, raking the sand and gravel ground, a little mowing between the barracks, physical training...anything to keep you occupied for several hours in a day. 'Policing' in this context: "...maintain order and neatness in (an area, as a military camp)," meaning to pick up litter and trash.

Every morning we assembled for formation...order our ranks (line up in equidistant rows) and be called to attention. With mind-numbing daily routine, roll call would be taken, uniforms and personal hygiene inspected, followed by morning assignments.

Typically formations were run by non commissioned officers (NCOs). Human nature, however, often dictates 'do less' rather than 'more,' so frequently the NCOs would delegate inspections and work assignments to lower ranking soldiers.

Enter Private First Class Bob

Bob... he was a 'first class' something all right, but as we got to know him better, it had little to do with his military rank. For some reason, two cosmic forces collided to bring us into proximity. He had a delayed class assignment, and he had caught the eye of the senior NCOs – meaning, they delegated some of the morning formation chores to him.

He seemed to relish finding inspection errors and, speaking for myself, he had a knack for assigning people – of his same rank – to tasks they particularly did NOT like. When my class assignment came, I was finished with Bob and could not have been more pleased!

After basic ATC it was off to Hunter Army Airfield in Savannah, Georgia for advanced training in radar approach control. In addition to a few hundred hours learning to guide helicopter pilots to a safe landings, I discovered that soldiers new to airfields were part of a broad practical joke conspiracy...sent on missions to retrieve buckets of 'prop wash' and yards of 'flight line.' Old hands seemed to never tire of sending earnest and naïve young men like me on these assignments. Everyone was in on it, so until someone took a little pity, it could go on for some time!!

For the uninitiated, prop wash is NOT something you use to clean the propellers of aircraft; rather the slipstream of air formed by their rotation, and flight line is NOT rope used to tie aircraft down in the wind, but the parking and servicing area for aircraft.

The training ended...

At Hunter, I got my orders for Vietnam. All of us knew we would be going, but when the actual orders arrived, it became real. We got a 30-day leave, a flight to Oakland, California and just like that, off to the war.

By the time I arrived in Vietnam, it had been several months and what seemed a lifetime from ATC School in Mississippi. Landing 'in-country,' was a little like getting to Keesler. I was put in a holding unit until orders came for duty station. It took a week or so, but arrive they did. I hitched a ride on a helicopter that made its way to Vung Tau Army Airfield, on the edge of a small peninsula slipping into the pristine waters of the South China Sea – my home for the next 13 months.

I got off the Huey chopper and headed for Base Operations to report for duty and get my assignment. The exact sequence of events is not clear, but while getting organized I heard a voice, "Hey Dreisinger!" That voice – it had a familiar and unpleasant ring to it - '...slowly I turned, step by step, inch by inch...,' and there he was - BOB!! He made some comment about the place, a familiar face, etc., etc., etc., ...All I could think of was, "Damn...Vietnam AND Bob!!"

Judging books and their covers

As disappointing as it was to see this guy, there was something different about him. He had an energy, drive and was missing the attitude I had so resented during the earlier days in Mississippi. He seemed genuinely pleased to see me!

You know how it is said, "... you may not be able to change your circumstances, but you can change the way you think about them." Maybe that was it, or maybe it was just a couple of young fellows a little afraid of the unknown with the slenderest common thread of experience.

I am not sure how our relationship evolved, but it did and fairly quickly. He was a tower controller and I worked radar from a small unit on the other side of the main runway. Often we worked the same shifts, and found ourselves grabbing chow together, playing a little basketball when off duty, exploring the surrounding peninsula, in spare time teaching English in a small school to Monks, children and prostitutes, taking R&R to Japan and Australia – and so many other things.

In that year little happened to one that did not happen to the other. In fact, his presence and friendship was so natural it seemed that it had always been. There was comfort in an implicit trust that developed between us. We became not just brothers in arms, but brothers in deed.

It's hard to express the fidelity – the love that grows between men when uncertain circumstances are shared; it is hard to express the loyalty that becomes ingrained; the growth and depth of understanding from unspoken words that take deep root. It is also hard to express how satisfying it is to be in an unconscious rhythm with another human being, that is so resonant nothing needs to be said...so it was with '...my first class friend...' Bob.

As the subsequent years unfolded, we found ourselves drifting in different directions and on to different lives. We lost touch off and on, but lately reconnected.

Yet, in the realm of the inexpressible, Bob – who at a certain time was the last human being I would ever have expected – became an icon of friendship, loyalty and love that remains ingrained in the depths of my heart and mind.

It is hard to imagine, as I look back on that period of my life, I would have survived without Bob at my side, but as he recently said in a brief note, "...we still had each other..."

Indeed we did Bob…in deeds we did.

A HOUSE IS NOT A HOME

"For in this we groan, earnestly desiring to be clothed
upon with our house which is from heaven.
If so be that being clothed we shall
not be found naked..."
- 2 Corinthians 5:2,3:
Bible

Everything was gone. The house was empty and yet it seemed smaller....

It had been a couple of months since last we saw one another, and while the movement of time had been the same for both of us, a universe of change had occurred. The inclination of descent into darkness seemed to have accelerated at a faster rate than I had expected.

My sister stays in an assisted living facility in Missouri. 'Assisted living'...that would be the broadest of ways to describe her place of residence. The wing where she lives is called "Harmony Hall," the portion of the facility where Alzheimer's patients find themselves.

Harmony Hall – the ultimate euphemism for confinement..."Oh yes, my loved one stays in Harmony Hall at the assisted living facility where she lives." It has an almost melodic ring, doesn't it?

While she is safe and well taken care of, 'harmony' is not the first word that comes to mind when visiting. She is the youngest person living in her unit, where all of the residents, to one degree or another, find themselves in diminishing worlds of reality – worlds of thought known only to themselves.

Leaving home

With her departure – when it became clear there would be no return – Nancy's home became simply a house; an empty space where a lifetime of personal things quite suddenly had no place...no context...nowhere to fit in. The photo's on the mantle, just photos – while familiar...the circumstance for their placement now missing, their meaning now unspoken.

The furniture arranged by a keen eye with a rationale...now just furniture. Little curiosities around the place, the kinds of personal little things we all gather in our lives, no longer having a story teller to advocate their meaning...now just curiosities. While her things were still in the house, there was a feeling of vacancy and a small but lingering sense of intrusion, brought about by her absence.

Once the course of no return was clear, the house would need to be cleaned up, cleared up and touched up to see if it could attract a new occupant who would have the opportunity to take possession; a new occupant who would have the opportunity to arrange *their* furniture...place *their* photos...put *their* little curiosities around, making this house...*their* home.

It's not that easy

None of this, of course, just happens. After all, when you go to the market place hoping someone will like you enough to take you on, you must be spruced up...you know, look your very best. Any house knows it cannot do it without help, so in come the workers and the task commences. Lots of things begin to happen...carpets removed...kitchen emptied of its appliances, cabinets, sink and flooring...bathroom fixture all gone...all gone.

Time for a fresh coat of paint, new carpet, appliances, flooring, bathroom fixtures...why if you didn't know it, you would have little idea these things had been done once before, when this structure had put on its best appearance longing to attract someone to its empty, sterile rooms, waiting...hoping to be occupied and changed from a house into a home. Someone did, and that someone was my sister...she made that house into *her* home.

It was a good run you know. That Nancy Jeanne knew how to turn a house…yes indeed, she knew how to bring love and joy and laughter, where nobody that walked through the door was a stranger…where hospitality began with a capital 'H' and ended with a capital 'Y!' It was the legacy under which she had been raised, and she carried the tradition with enthusiasm. She had the kind of charisma that willed the four walls of that house to be a home…her home and anyone else's who happened to be visiting. Yes, it was a damn fine home and a damn fine run wasn't it?…wasn't it?

It *was* fine…wasn't it?

That was then
Now they both sit waiting.

One with hope to once again be filled with ornaments in its nooks and crannies – making it unique and different, given new life by its new occupant…hoping to become a home once again. For you see, houses don't always become homes…sometimes they just remain houses. A house doesn't always get the opportunity to become a home.

The other? Ah yes the other. She just waits. She had that special gift…she knew the secret that making a house a home was a collaboration between the two…you couldn't just buy a place and move in…there was more, so much more. She understood it took love and elbow grease to transform and give that building personality…life…light…you know…make it a home!!

But now her time seems to have passed, so she sits in her little room in Harmony Hall and waits…a bed, a comfortable chair, a wide screen television, a common gathering area just down the hall from that little room where there are…well, things to do, food to eat and "…others who in one degree or another, find themselves in diminishing worlds of reality – worlds of thought known only to themselves…."

Yes indeed, there are secrets in so many of those minds – secrets that were exercised in vibrancy and energy and focus and productivity and love and laughter – that are increasingly locked away as they wait…as their loved ones wait…relegated to brief, shallow monologues hoping to elicit a glimpse of the world that once was, the paradise lost.

Is there meaning?
Empty houses reflect two possibilities – the coming and the going. One a 'hello,' and the other a 'good-bye'…the 'hello' filled with an anticipation

of challenge and excitement… the 'good-bye,' a bit of sadness and melancholy at the inevitability of change.

My sister's home has become a house as surely as her mind has begun to slip away toward an unknown place of residence. Her '…furniture, fixtures and curiosities…' seem to have lost their context…so she waits. Almost everything is gone, and of little doubt, she seems much smaller.

Somehow though, I believe she still has a secret up her sleeve; somehow I believe she knows there is a new home waiting for her special touch – her gift; somehow I believe she knows…

How could I not?

IN FACT THERE ARE FEW

"If you love somebody tell them...
better yet, show them!"
- Anonymous

It was a Tuesday afternoon when Mattie Belzer took her last breath, and one of the gentlest souls I have ever known in my life ended this part of her journey. She and I were more than friends. I suppose, other than my mother, Mattie was one of the most gentle and generous souls I ever knew. It was a painful loss.

We met when I began attending a small Bible teaching ministry in the heartland of this country – Mattie was one of the elders in the group. What began as a temporary church home, turned into more than 30 years, filled with some of the most interesting and meaning experiences of my life.

During those years I finished university, taught in university, and entered the professional world of chronic back and neck pain. The work in spine put food on the table, but it was not the central focus of my life. On the motorcycle speeding down the highway of life, it was nothing more than a sidecare.

I thought I had found my life's work and would end my years teaching the scriptures and ministering to others who like me, shared uncertainties of the universe. I had slipped underground, off the grid, picked up a shovel and begun digging to find meaning in life. Mattie was an anchor...a lifeline tossed just at the right moment...a piece of solid ground upon which to stand in the shifting sands of a young life.

Getting there

I had come back from the war, probably a little more troubled than I was willing to admit. In those days, when unsettled, I got busy...you know time and mind occupying activities to stay the tide, plug the dyke, withhold the fear, hide from the madding crowd...treading water in the sea of life trying to make sense of it all...or maybe just a little.

Undergraduate school in West Virginia had unexpectedly come along, followed by graduate work in Wisconsin – all of it structured and mind occupying. After finishing both degrees, I was faced with the same dilemma...you know, the meaning part. Don't think too much, just work. Fortunately, there was another degree to complete before having to face...well...face life. It was in Missouri where it all began to catch up with me.

There were a couple of years left in the doctoral program, things were slowing down a little and I could no longer avoid the call. It had been a good run, but the secret had been revealed...one could not educate themselves into contentment. Of the gold rings on the carousel of life, the reality did not match the expectation.

More knowledge? Surely. Answers? There were few! The great metaphor in my life reflected in the voice of the 1960s torch singer Peggy Lee from the Leiber and Stoller lyric:

> "Is that all there is, is that all there is
> If that's all there is my friends, then let's keep dancing
> Let's break out the booze and have a ball
> If that's all there is..."

What's the point? Is there meaning?

It had a beginning

It was a chilly spring evening in late April or Early May of 1975 when I met Dick. A friend had been trying to introduce us for some time, suggesting he was a little strange...like me. She thought maybe he and I might find some resonance. We did meet...we did resonate and there was little doubt he was – we were – different...that meeting and subsequent events changed the course of my life forever.

Mattie – words mean so little

Dick introduced me to a Biblical teaching ministry and as part of it I met Mattie B., a woman in her fifties, who touched my life in ways no other had before or since. I do not have the vocabulary to describe this Missouri country woman, whose exposure to the world at large was very small; whose education was minimal; whose early life had been lived on a rural farm...BUT whose heart was of galactic proportion.

Mattie was a peculiar woman. Her voice gravely...speech plain spoken and direct...her inner ears had been damaged, so she heard through a sound conduction device resting on the mastoid bone located just behind her left earlobe – looking like her head phone was out of place...behind the ear rather than on it. She kept the pick up microphone clipped to her bra, so sometimes you had to speak into her chest for her to understand you...to the uninitiated onlooker, particularly new people visiting church – a strange and sometimes disquieting sight.

She was partially blind in one eye and ultimately would have it replaced with an artificial one. She played the tuba in church and what she lacked in musical training – which was in fact non-existent – she made up for with spiritual enthusiasm. Sometimes the spirit would inspire her to preach in church, and when she did there was indeed a '...mighty rushing wind...'

She was one of the elder mothers of this rural ministry, and as such taught the scripture, counseled younger members, and did what she did best...led by example. She worked in the church office, spending thousands of hours typing the scriptures and checking concordances for accuracy. She was a pretty good cook, as long as it was solid country food...meat, corn bread, vegetables and potatoes...none of that, you know "...fancy stuff..."

She may not have had the educational, economic or social access dangled in front of us by the pressures of life, but whatever gifts she had been given she exercised to maximal potential. You knew where she stood, and if she loved you there was nothing...there was 'no thing' that could separate you from it, and while I was not the only one...there was little doubt she loved me!

Over the years, this woman cut my hair, taught me, counseled and inspired me when times seemed darkest...a beacon of unwavering faith that appeared at the time, and until her death, bottomless.

None of this, however, tells even part of the story of who or what this woman was in my life. Faith? Honor? Justice? Her life defined them. Love? Compassion? Thoughtfulness? All of that and more.

Her sense of humor...beyond belief. Much of the laughter came from her plainness of speech and use of whatever word worked for her in the moment – exactly correct or not. Her directness of speech came without the social filters most of us are taught and brought with it at times an unspeakable joy.

As the years moved forward, this woman had health challenges that would stop even the strongest of character. The loss of sight in one eye and greatly reduced vision in the other and increasing deafness making it more difficult to hear – diabetes contributing to both. She was married to a fellow who spent more time away from home than not…and yet, and yet through all of this she gave everything she had to others…always to others…to me.

Her life was the antithesis of the Leiber and Stoller existential lyric. She understood almost by instinct this life was only a preparation…really not much more. Her life was not one of angst informed by 'great thinkers' working to solve the mysteries of life. She had faith…she lived in the moment…what more could one ask or do?

The debt

How does one repay unconditional love from another human being? How does one balance the books in relationships where there are no expectations, no desire for recompense, no pressure, not a whisper of a quid pro quo? How does one express the influence another has had on their life when it comes with no strings attached? The answer, of course, is one cannot repay…there is no balancing of the books…there is, in the end, doing one's best to live to her example.

In life, if one were brutally honest, there are few who bring these things to the table. In my life, Mattie was, without question or doubt, one of those.

In the end, before that Tuesday afternoon during a routine echocardiogram when Mattie gasped with surprise and took her last breath, I had moved to Michigan and we had lost the intimate contact we had had for so many years. This gentle soul who had invested so much in me slipped quietly home, as the scripture says, "…to a place she had never been before…"

OPEN THE DOOR, OR AT LEAST CONSIDER IT

> "I took the road less traveled by, and
> that made all the difference."
> - Frost, R

"I'm okay. This top and bottom will wick water away from my body."

It didn't seem to matter that she was wearing a sleeveless pink tank top and below the knee black tights. She had never been to the desert. She had traveled some in her young life, but Detroit had not prepared her for the heat and barrenness of the Anza Boregga desert in the fall. I talked her into putting on a light colored long-sleeve shirt and a funky looking wide-brimmed hat to discourage the relentless work the sun from sucking her body water to quickly.

The temperature was over 100F (37.7C) as we started into the canyon. The hike covered 3 miles (4.8km) along a dry riverbed over moderately rough terrain. Our goal? An oasis buried in the canyon. When the rains come, this river wash is filled with treacherous waters collected from the surrounding mountainsides...the occasional large palm tree trunk lying along the way...a testament to nature's power.

We were carrying a half-gallon (1.9 liters) of water in hydration packs on our backs, but a Desert Police Officer we met near the trail head suggested we go back to town and pick up another half gallon each.

"This hike is going to take you more than two hours," she said. "You're starting late; it will be hot. Go get a little more water." So we did.

The unguarded moment...
"Hi, my name is Joanna," came an unfamiliar voice on the phone.

"I'm a friend of Scott's. We met a few months ago at a Detroit Shock (women's professional team) basketball game. Would you be interested in acting as a mentor for me?"

"I don't know," I said, caught a little off-guard. "Why don't we grab a cup of coffee and see what happens."

In truth, I couldn't remember having met her.

A brief interlude...
Scott S. was a young man who came into my life through a colleague from Longwood, Florida. Scott was head strength coach for one of the universities in Detroit, and an unusual young man...unusual because after college, he dedicated nearly a decade of his life to self-education.

By the time we met, he had read over 3,000 books on motivation and philosophy. He had watched countless films and videos about the lives of successful athletes and other social notables. He kept diligent notes, copied sayings and success stories, creating a formidable library. We resonated immediately and met bi-monthly for coffee early on Saturday mornings. During one of these visits he told me he would be leaving the university for a position in Tampa, Florida. I had gotten used to our meetings and was saddened to see him go.

Coffee no – tea yes...
Joanna and I agreed on a place and a time to see whether we thought we might be able to dance a little. We met and scoped each other out. It didn't take much time before we knew this would not be our first/last meeting. There was just something about her that was compelling.

And so bi-weekly meetings that began at an Einstein's Bagel shop has lasted...except for some time intervals, travel and change of location...until this present time. There were a few notable differences in the beginning that have remained: I drink coffee and she tea; our age difference is 37 years, I am Caucasian and she African American...all of that, as it turns out...nothing more than background noise.

I've mentored a number of people over the years, but few like Joanna. It was clear from the start she was very bright, but was also passionate...engaged...eager ...focused and hungry to absorb everything she could. It was clear that in her mind failure on life's journey was NOT an option. She was on a deliberate mission to gather whatever tools it would take to succeed.

When Molly and I moved out West, Joanna and I remained in contact as she finished her Masters in Business Administration and hunted relentlessly for work in a city where the automobile industry had dominated everything. The recession wounded Detroit badly, but she knew if given a chance, there would be no stopping her.

Let's see, where were we...
Oh yes, the desert! The hike ended up being excellent...the advice from our officer friend proved valuable...I drank nearly the full gallon of water during the trip into and out of the canyon. We enjoyed each other's company the easy way friends do...for my mentoring capacity had been drained. Now it was just 'us.'

This hike was an oddly crafted metaphor...a reflection of the rare gift of our friendship. On the way in, we came around a large rock. Less than 10 feet in front of us stood a male Bighorn sheep...alone and majestically regal – a sight not often seen. Happening upon this ram, was as surprisingly unlikely as the connection this young woman and I had forged over coffee and tea on Saturday mornings in Detroit.

A little reflection...
This was Joanna's third visit with us in California, and it would be the last for a while. She got that entry level job as a buyer for a large diesel engine company owned by Daimler in Germany, and after a little more than two years on the job was promoted to senior buyer and moved to Germany for three years at corporate offices.

There are few things in life that give one greater pleasure than friendships. They begin because people find something good in one another...something that resonates...something timeless...something not clearly describable – ageless, race-less, and yes, even drink-less (coffee/tea).

When that call comes from an unfamiliar voice, as many have for all of us, take a moment to consider it, for it is written, "Be not forgetful to entertain strangers: for thereby some have entertained angels unawares."

"Hi, my name is Joanna," came an unfamiliar voice on the phone.

We met for coffee and an angel came into our lives.

UNEXPECTED MEMORIES

> "Memory…the diary we all carry with us."
> - Oscar Wilde

I hate being late!!

It was close to 9AM, driving on East McCarty street in Jefferson City, Missouri and I was running a little late to the bank. I had set the meeting a week earlier before leaving San Diego to take care of some family business while visiting with my sister. The appointment had been set, it was clear I wouldn't quite make it on time, and for a fellow who doesn't like to be late…I was a little stressed.

Memories built…

You know how it is when you are doing something sort of mindlessly…listening to music, exercising, driving a car…when suddenly a memory pops into your head. The trigger could be anything – often unknown. A memory that you could not have brought to mind if someone had given you money, but there it is, clear as day!

An odd little place…

As fate would have it, I passed the address where Molly and I had first lived after getting married. It had been an odd little three-room apartment along the length of half the building with rooms stacked end to end…living room, bedroom and kitchen next to one another in a straight line. Getting to the kitchen, in the back, meant passing through the bedroom in the middle – the bathroom just off the kitchen. Because the bathroom was just off the kitchen, visitors needing to use it had to go through the bedroom.

Passing that address on East McCarty Street triggered one of those remembrances that bubbled up in my brain until I laughed out loud. It didn't matter that the building was now gone, replaced by an empty lot! My mind instantly returned to the apartment with its appearance and 'feel' in intimate detail. Moments like this remind me what a wondrous gift we have as human beings to be able to recall both images and feelings…even smells and sensations.

Dick had a place…

Off and on we had a good friend stay with us. Since we had no spare room, Dick slept on the couch in the living room. He and I had started a small consulting business and ran an early morning – 5AM – community fitness program. Later, in the not too distant future, he would move to Jefferson City, but in the meantime, the couch was the best we had to offer.

This led to curious privacy issues, because in the night, if he needed to use the facilities, he had to pass through our bedroom. Usually, I was asleep, but occasionally, I would wake up and see this dark figure tiptoeing quietly through the room like the spectre in the Scottish marshes. One particular night, both Molly and I noticed this and got the giggles. The kind of giggles that are hard to stop once they get going. Dick trying to quietly slip through… the two of us trying to ignore the fact he was going just by the bed…in a moment, the three of us were in stitches…I suppose you would had to have been there, but it was funny!

As I drove by the address on that Monday morning, I was instantly transported to the image of this event and saw it as clearly as if it had just happened!

Who knows how it works…

In the Bible David writes: "…for I am fearfully and wonderfully made: marvellous are thy works; and that my soul knoweth right well." (Psalm 139:14)

While we live in an animal body – wondrous in its own right – it is the mind that has such an astonishing and apparently unlimited capacity.

It doesn't take much reflection to appreciate almost everything we use in our lives came from an idea in someone's mind. Things we take for granted in every day life – from the tiny and intricate to the large and complex – began somewhere in the recesses of someone's mind as a simple thought…a simple "…'hmm, I wonder'…'what if?" – an awesome thing to appreciate.

It would be enough if we had only the capacity to create things from thought and the resources we find around us, but there is more. David writes in another place: "When I consider thy heavens, the work of thy fingers, the moon and the stars, which thou hast ordained; What is man, that thou art mindful of him?..." (Psalm 8:3,4). We have the capacity to reflect and wonder about the grander and unknown things beyond...you know...just beyond the unseen horizon. It is the '...just beyond...' that really drives, or rather draws us.

Yet, this mind, this curious and for the most part poorly understood mass of protoplasm, protected and locked inside the hard case of our skull, also has the capacity to simply entertain us. I don't mean entertain in the broader sense...theater, art, film, song, or dance...I mean just in quiet, maybe even intimate moments when we least expect it. You know, like driving past a place thirty years in the past and having a crystal clear memory come back...back to remind...back to reflect...back to bring context...back to bring a chuckle or maybe just because!

A momentary step aside…

I know this memory thing can work with reminders that are sometimes painful and not so pleasant. I also know that when any thought instantly returns to our minds, we can embrace or reject it...we can open the door to further reflection or close it and move on. I believe this kind of conscious acceptance and rejection helps to shape the going forward in our lives.

Back on task…

On this morning as I hurried, late and stressed to make a meeting, I was given the unrequested gift of an event in life that provided exactly what I needed to bring a little relief, perspective and appreciation. Yeah, I made the meeting...a little late, but in the few minutes it took to get there, I was reminded not just of an event, but a part of the rich fabric of my life, the people in it and the journey that has made it so meaningful this far....

I DON'T KNOW...DO YOU?

"Knowing others requires paying attention,
paying attention takes time..."
- anonymous

I have a niece, Mariah, with whom I have the most rewarding of relationships. When she was a little girl we found a rhythm...a special place really, where I suppose we just knew each other...maybe it is that we wanted to know each other. I can't remember having a forced conversation, or that I felt obligated to carry the conversation...somehow, from very early on it just 'was.' At the age of 28 (hers) the only thing that has changed is the content and cadence, but not that connection...

This leads to the confession meant to dispel the myth young people have of their elders...maybe just older people. The myth? That somehow with age comes 'the' understanding of life. You know...somehow older folk have figured it out.

When I was young, my father was bigger than life...a giant, not just in size, but it seemed he knew EVERYTHING. While I was trying to figure life out, it was clear to me that he already knew all the answers. I felt this way because there was almost never a hesitation in his responses to my questions, given with a sense of assurance, that made me look forward to becoming just like him.

As life rushed at me with the speed of light, the challenges a little more complicated, the aura of my dad remained...better said, and this is key, I kept the aura of him in my mind. An image...and like the images we often create in our minds it was simplified and tucked away in the '...secure place...' the '...this is the way things are...' room. Often once the image is stored, it becomes a static file...a 'byte' of information requiring deliberate events to be updated. Updating an image of one's father or mother or anyone for that matter, takes time...perspective...a different place in the journey.

Briefly during my teenage years, you know, the era of ultimate enlightenment and raging hormones, this image got updated – rather downgraded. I was pretty sure my dad, for all his assurance really didn't know very much...his 'bandwidth' seemed to be pretty thin. I mean, when you now realize you understand most things, parents are so...so, you know – yesterday!

Then somewhere in my mid-twenties, after the Vietnam experience, my dad got pretty smart again. I had more unresolved questions, and what seemed quite sudden; his bandwidth appeared to have grown exponentially. His thoughts were richer...his understanding deeper...his sense of life more thoughtful. In many ways, in spite of having outgrown him by seven full inches, he became even bigger than before.

But then something else began to happen...I got into my late 30s and discovered life was not as clear as it had seemed in my teens and twenties – the answers I had relied on, less and less secure...and my dad? He had become ill and seemed more uncertain of the answers he had given to me as a youngster, teen and young adult.

My father looked less a giant with a never-ending wealth of knowledge and understanding of life...morphing into something different, something more...a human being. The paradox – maybe the revelation – from this point on the pathway of life changed the view. Now his humanity, his failing health, his diminished capacity, and slipping away from the vitality and power of his life, upgraded the image from a series of 'still photos' to a moving picture – like the rapid flipping of pictures that make images appear alive and moving. The words of the apostle Paul took on a sense of meaning for the first time – "...when I am weak, then am I strong..."

My father had entered into life just like his son...grasping at whatever seemed consistent and secure. I realized – maybe with purpose...maybe not – he had created a barrier to his humanity, or maybe better said, I had created a barrier to it through the snapshots I had tucked away in the reference library of my mind. At the very time he was slipping away, I had the intense desire to know him better. In truth, it would be years after his death while reading the dozens and dozens of letters he wrote, for me to get better insight into this man.

The niece...

You see, in the middle of my sixth decade, I really don't know much more than I did when I was in my first few. I've learned to recognize some patterns to life and figured out how to find a little order in the chaos. I appreciate, with greater respect, the fragility of the journey with little guarantee of the next breath.

One thing I do know, however, is that I have worked diligently to keep whatever image my niece has of me in her mind, as fluid as possible. I have tried to ensure she knows my humanity, my misgivings, my sense of the great unknown...I want to make whatever journey we have together just that...together. I want her to see me as she sees herself...curious, frail, thoughtful, full of wonderment, with a sense of the microcosmic space we inhabit and the macrocosmic capacity for unlimited possibility.

Indeed, it is my hope for those who have known me that their images are moving and nuanced...not simply 'still photos.'

SPEED CAN SLOW YOU DOWN

> "The faster I go, the behinder I get."
> - Lewis Carroll

We were wandering home after the movie, and had taken one of the side roads to avoid the Interstate. As I looked in my rearview mirror, there was a woman driving a late model Mazda tailing me close enough to have warranted a dinner invitation, had we been able to speak. I politely tapped my brakes to let her know I wasn't sure we knew each other quite well enough to be...how should I put it politely...nearly so intimate with one another.

The last section of this bypass is four-lane, so as soon as we got to that point, she zoomed by me, giving me 'the look.' Off she went like the rabbit in Aesop's fable <u>The Tortoise and the Hare</u>, and slipped out of site. I was thinking as she went by, "go for it lady."

Justice for the tortoise came as a result of the hare's belief the turtle was no competition. But the tortoise just kept plodding along, and as the story goes, crossed the finish line first! The moral? Well there are a couple of them.

<u>Tortoise</u>: When in the arena, stay in there, don't give up, keep at it, and be steady.

<u>Hare</u>: No matter what one thinks of their skill set, one must 'be' and 'stay' in the arena. Confidence, dare I say overconfidence, must be matched with action.

Justice in my case came a little more quickly in the form of a stoplight. Rounding the corner, there she was waiting at a red light. As I pulled up behind her, I snuggled my car close to the back of hers. She glanced up. She had blown by me because she was in a hurry, but here we were, together at the stoplight…ah, the stoplight…the great equalizer. We shared a brief 'rear view mirror' moment, smiled – both 'getting it' – and as the light turned green went on with our day. Okay, I did feel a little satisfaction – this time. I smiled again reminding myself how often I had been the one in a hurry, only to find myself sharing the stoplight with the person I had passed.

It doesn't take much happening around me to get small take-aways from events in my life. Hurrying up, doesn't always get one there faster, and taking one's time doesn't always make one late. I was reminded Lewis of Carroll's great lines in <u>Through the Looking Glass</u>. Alice had been running with the Queen, and when she stopped noticed she was in the same place as where she had started:

"Well, in our country," said Alice, still panting a little, "you'd generally get to somewhere else -- if you ran very fast for a long time, as we've been doing."

"A slow sort of country!" said the Queen. "Now, here, you see, it takes all the running you can do, to keep in the same place. If you want to get somewhere else, you must run at least twice as fast as that!"

Then I thought about the unavoidable BIG STOPLIGHT at the end of our journey, and all the little stoplights along the way. I thought about how it is we occupy ourselves and how, in the moment, we feel things to be so important, that we must 'get there quickly.' AND yet, in the end, we all find ourselves at the same intersection. That caused me to smile a little too.

It's how we live our life that counts. If we hurry, hurry, hurry, we run the risk of missing a lot along the way. If we do nothing, we run the risk of, well…doing nothing.

Getting older has its benefits and liabilities. The benefit is a richer understanding of the importance of appreciating small moments and finding meaning in them. The liability, at least for me, is that it has taken many years to find the proper pace.

"Youth wasted on the young?" Maybe…but then again, letting those speeders slip by while focusing on the things that are important to us…is not so bad. Let them go, because, an energetic push to 'get there' frequently keeps one from appreciating the journey.

You know, "...it's not the destination, but..." finding the proper speed.

THE BEST IS FREE

"Time to get up…time to wake up…
time to get up in the morning.
Time to end rest…time for our best…
time to get up in the morning…"
- Anonymous

A humming bird was quietly investigating the grapefruit tree, Texas Ranger bush and long past flowering buds of the barrel cactus in the yard. Dove and quail were 'singing in' the new day as they and the rest of the desert wild life woke to spend their coming hours foraging for, or becoming another creature's, daily fare.

The moon was still clear in the sky above the clouds moving in on the eastern horizon - the air a little heavy, for the desert, as monsoon season would bring afternoon rains. Even in the desert there is an unmistakable clean and refreshing smell – you can almost feel – when the rains come.

There is something about watching the curtain rise in the darkened theater of the Sonoran Desert. At first everything is the same color, as though the normally functioning eye is totally colorblind.

Then, in the subtlest of ways, a salmon wisp of color tinges the bottom of a barely discernable stratus cloud appearing strung out like a malformed piece of cloth in the northeastern sky. It appears visually as one might imagine the 'first chair' violin sets the tuning note for an orchestra preparing to play.

With its appearance, other clouds become visible in the eastern sky, grey and apparently ominous above the Catalina mountains....BUT then....then as the first act opens, a huge sheet of stratus clouds, as though waiting for their cue, begin to emerge with brilliant pinks and then reds controlled by some unseen hand on the rheostat of the universe. For the briefest of moments it holds the eye and mind, both wishing it would stay just as it is.

Again as if on cue, these clouds lose their color...now appearing grey...now white for the day as they move on and morph and dissipate and build, precursors for the coming cumulonimbus storm clouds following their scent.

The color show ends with a large and dense block of clouds lighted in the yellowish tinge one sees in the night sky when a city's electric landscape provides a signpost of its presence beneath a darkened sky.

Soon, the morning concert ends and all the lighter weight clouds become whitish wraiths in the fully lit morning sky...the more dense of the bunch remaining "...50 shades of grey..." undefined by human behavior, but rather by the master conductor. One cannot help but be taken by the amazing cycle of life that begins anew each day.

We have been blessed with two gifts – one of which is to see what happens to the things around us, and how they appear to interact. The other is to have the ability as a spectator of life, to be grateful for it.

We have an animal body, not terribly unlike the bodies of all other living creatures. We eat, sleep, protect ourselves and procreate our species, then cycle off the planet as any other body does. In this respect we are no different than the beast.

We also have, however, the ability to understand and use that understanding to appreciate life around us.

We have binocular sight to navigate our world, but there is more. God has made color and texture that permits us to appreciate our sight...not simply as a tool for survival and navigation, but rather for understanding. If all of the objects in our universe fell outside of the frequency with which we see, we would not know they were there and what would be the point.

It is not the clouds in the sky that make the music, but the processing mind that is given to appreciate its meaning.

While there is much in common that we have with the irrational, survival based creatures of the earth, we have the ability to understand…to seek…to learn, for it is one thing to see and use something, it is another to understand…and that can take a lifetime of quiet consideration.

It is written, "Wisdom is the principle thing, therefore get wisdom, but with all thy getting, get understanding…"

"A humming bird was quietly investigating the grapefruit tree…" and I continue to pray for understanding….

TIME TO START LIVING

> "Life isn't about finding yourself,
> it's about creating yourself."
> - George Bernard Shaw

It's quiet in the mornings when I get out of bed. I try to remember to say, "Thank you" as I put my feet on the floor – one word for each foot...I try to...

My friend Frank uses the shower as a reminder of the blessings in his life, with something like, "Thank you God for the gifts you have given me. Help me be a better man."

The thing is, we are a couple of older guys who try to look at life as though we were young guys. While there is little doubt the end of the story is much closer than the beginning, AND there is little doubt there are a few more aches and pains, we still express gratitude for what has been and look forward to being better as life continues to rush toward us.

Perspective and the journey...
Gail and I were talking about this a couple of days ago. She is a neighbor who has retired from a successful working life, but continues to ask the questions and seek the answers related to, "What's next?"

There is, after all the small "...what's next..." and in a cosmic sense the bigger "...WHAT'S NEXT?!"

One has to do with what is coming in the short term and the

other? While I have certain confidences, I am uncertain about the details…

In the small ball of '…what's next…' I am graduating from giving scientific/clinical talks to local lectures related to life and imagination.

That's right – graduating!

There are a few items on the horizon related to my professional journey, but as life moves forward, a need to connect with people in my local community has grown considerably.

Teaching a workshop…

These issues are on the top of my mind, because I prepared and taught a workshop this week called Life Reimagined for the American Association of Retired People (AARP). I took the course last year and decided to become certified as a 'guide' for others who have an interest in resetting their imaginations as a guidepost for the future.

You remember your imagination, right? That indefinable thing that emerges early in life after the 'starter dough' of faith and curiosity have taken root. Once we get enough experience, that is to say enough vocabulary of life experience, our little minds begin to entertain the possibilities of what's next.

It has to start somewhere…

My first realization of possibility happened because of television. Watching sports, I made the decision I would be a professional athlete - I was probably five or six.

"Daddy, when I grow up, I'm going to be a professional athlete." I said with great seriousness.

"In the summer, I will play for the Cleveland Indians…in the fall for the Cleveland Browns and in the spring for the Boston Celtics!"

Bob Feller pitched for the Indians, I was pretty sure the 'Browns' were named after Jim Brown, and was there a better basketball player than Bob Cousy of the Boston Celtics?

"Honey," my father replied, "you can be whatever you want to be."

As fate, talent and circumstance would happen, my imagined successes on the field, gridiron and court never emerged.

I had to re-imagine my future as life moved forward.

This week...

Friday morning, 15 upper middle-aged folk made their way into the classroom at the local library to see what this Life Reimagined thing was all about.

Since I had actually never taught this course before, I began, "These are the words you never want to hear when you get on an airplane. This is my first flight!"

In a nutshell, the program provides tools to help people get unstuck when their lives have stalled because of personal tragedy, loss of a loved one, retirement, or just a need to find structure to move forward...not solutions, but direction.

Life has moments when we feel comfortable, a place that is familiar and a rhythm that seems to work. Life, however, IS change! Nothing ever stays the same – from the size of our feet...clothing...shifting work life...growing families...everything!

Life is unpredictable, and in the words and music of Stephen Schwartz for the Broadway musical Pippin – *No time at all* – originally sung by Irene Ryan (Ma Clampett in television's Beverly Hillbillies):

> *"Before it's too late stop trying to wait*
> *For fortune and fame you're secure of*
> *For there's <u>one thing to be sure of</u>, mate:*
> *<u>There's nothing to be sure of!</u>"*

The Life Reimagined workshop is a couple of hours dedicated to reflecting about past life accomplishments and the imagination and effort they required. It is a program using these experiences to remind people they were once driven by their imagination and while life may have taken a toll, their imaginations were still intact...their lives, going forward were about 'reimagining' what they would like to be doing, and a reminder of the skill sets they already had.

One might say the watchwords for this course could be found in the chorus of that Broadway song:

Oh, it's time to start livin'
Time to take a little from this world we're given
Time to take time, cause spring will turn to fall
In just no time at all....

Event complete – life continued...

In the end, the 'first flight' went well for all of us. In many ways, it brought together for me, all of the life communication skills I have developed and an appreciation for just how similar all of us – every single one of us – are.

I can't say what the impact of the experience had on all of the attendees, but a room that began with 15 strangers, finished with a group who felt their lives were anything but over...a room of fellow travelers who had made lists of small accomplishable things they could begin almost immediately...a room of people who realized they were not the only ones feeling the sense of free floating anxiety, wondering what's next?

Gratitude...you bet!

When I got out of bed the next morning, 'Thank you" seemed particularly meaningful. When I got out of bed, I thought about Frank's words and was more thankful for the gifts I have been given...when I got out of bed I felt more strongly how much I want to continue to become a better man...

OVER ALMOST BEFORE IT STARTS

"They lose the day in expectation of the night,
and night in fear of the dawn."
- Lucius Annaeus Seneca,
On the Shortness of Life

I've been thinking about dying lately.

I'm actually kinda looking forward to it.

These thoughts have nothing to do with big disappointments in life, or accelerating the time course, or hoping for an unexpected event that might end it all…lights out…the big sleep…a one way ticket to ride.

They have nothing to do with hoping I will not end up in an extended care facility rocking back and forth until my last breath, nor struggling through a terminal chronic disease, robbing me of all self respect and awareness. All of that is an uncertain and totally unpredictable fantasy of the future.

Death is not the fantasy, but spending time in fear of what might happen truly is…

Truth? We have no guarantee of tomorrow…

These thoughts have been more along the lines of knowing the time 'working for the company' is not permanent and within the constraints of my own expectations and desires, trying to get as much out of the ride as is possible.

178

Life passes so quickly, we often miss doing things we meant to and find ourselves immersed in thoughts of regret...robbing us of the moment we are in. It is easy to fall into a mind-set that 'time and gravity' have taken more than they have given.

The thing is that from the moment we take our first breath and enter the theater of life 'stage right,' all signs point toward the exit 'stage left.' This is simply the natural order of things...there is no eternal youth, no magic potion, no 'deal with the devil' that gives eternal youth in exchange for our soul. We are, as Mark Aurelius was fond of saying, "...but a small wet spot..." who should get up every morning and fully live the life of a human being – whatever that means for us!

In the end, I suppose it is all about the way we view life and the decisions we make on a daily basis (minute by minute really). Importantly, it is never too late to do things now rather than putting them off.

Country music lyricists and musicians Tim Nichols and Craig Wiseman, in a song recorded by country artist Tim McGraw, sum it up best in their pop culture piece "Live like you were dying."

...I loved deeper,
And I spoke sweeter,
And I gave forgiveness I've been denying,
And he said someday I hope you get the chance,
To live like you were dyin'.

The Roman poet Horace (Odes) provided the frequently used phrase – "Carpe Diem" (seize the day). I like a modification of that phrase sent to me by a friend: "Carpe the heck out of the Diem."

Nichols and Wiseman were right, we should do our best to "...live like [we are] dyin'..."

'Cause we are...and that is not a bad thing....

Other published work by Ted Dreisinger

'life in small bites – moments in time…' - 2014

Available at Amazon.com in paperback and Kindle

www.ingramcontent.com/pod-product-compliance
Lightning Source LLC
Chambersburg PA
CBHW032033040426
42449CB00007B/878